SECOND EDITION

STATECRAFT
AND
STAGECRAFT

AMERICAN POLITICAL LIFE IN THE AGE OF PERSONALITY

ROBERT SCHMUHL

STATECRAFT AND STAGECRAFT:

AMERICAN POLITICAL LIFE
IN THE AGE OF PERSONALITY

Library of Congress Cataloging-in-Publication Data

Schmuhl, Robert.
    Statecraft and stagecraft : American political life in the
age of personality / Robert Schmuhl. — 2nd ed.
        p.   cm.
    Includes bibliographical references.
    ISBN 0-268-01744-1 (pbk.)
    1. Mass media — Political aspects — United States.
2. United States — Politics and government — 1981-1989.
3. United States — Politics and government — 1989-
I. Title.
P95.82.U6S35   1992
302.23'0973 — dc20   91-44655
                                                                              CIP

Statecraft
and
Stagecraft:
American Political Life in the Age of Personality

Robert Schmuhl

UNIVERSITY OF NOTRE DAME PRESS
NOTRE DAME   LONDON

FOR JUDY

Contents

Preface

A few months before his death in 1961, James Thurber began an essay about the relationship between politics and entertainment by writing: "History is replete with proofs, from Cato the Elder to Kennedy the Younger, that if you scratch a statesman you find an actor, but it is becoming harder and harder, in our time, to tell government from show business."

As Thurber notes, the interplay between political acting and performing for the public extends back in time as far as a historian — or humorist — can see. In recent years, the lines between statecraft and stagecraft have faded to the point that the two now blur together. A legacy of the Reagan presidency is the lesson that statecraft can be enhanced through stagecraft. For eight years, political action and public policy followed not only briefing books but scripts. Substance coexisted with a style of presentation that effectively exploited the dramatic values of the various sources of popular communication responsible for covering the White House.

Ronald Reagan rarely missed a cue, but it is wrong to think that the drawing together of statecraft and stagecraft resulted from having an actor elected president. The linkage between public policy and public performance for a mass audience has a rich heritage in twentieth-century American political history. Theodore Roosevelt commanded the silver screen in the early days of the movies, and Franklin Roosevelt chatted with a nation via the radio. Videogenic, image-sensitive John Kennedy pioneered the use of television in conducting public affairs, and twenty years later Reagan raised that use to an art form. Reagan also refused to abandon his professional roots. The old sports announcer con-

ducted a weekly radio program of plain talk about his perspec-
tives and proposals for a national audience.

The Reagan years magnified the relationship between statecraft and stagecraft. That relationship, however, grows out of a
sociocultural climate that is dramatically different from what it
was just three decades ago. Since the 1960s, modes of popular
communication, especially television, have grown in significance,
influencing all aspects of American life. The political world — of
campaigning and governing, of civic participation and public
discourse — is one conspicuous area, and the territory of this book.
This area — where statecraft encompasses both seeking public office and formal governmental conduct — is, in large measure, a
reflection of the broader, media-obsessed culture. To talk of "the
mediaization of American politics," as some commentators do,
might offend the sensibilities of those who admire stately and
graceful phrases. However, the phenomenon so barbarously described is taking place and warrants sustained scrutiny.

Shortly before he died in 1986, Theodore H. White, chroni-
cler of president-making, observed that contemporary politics in
the United States had become "videotropic." Like heliotropic
plants that need sun to live, public figures today require the light
of television for political life. White's metaphor is useful as we
look beyond television's artificial light to see how the whole environment of popular communications interacts with and affects
our political world.

The influence of the media far exceeds an ability to speak in
quotable aphorisms or (for males) to observe a dress code of dark
suit, blue shirt, and red tie. The values of popular communication take hold, too, leading to an emphasis on appealing images,
symbolic gestures, dramatic encounters, audience-gathering opportunities. Such an environment places a premium on personality, with the personality often taking precedence over political
beliefs, principles, and policies.

Given the characteristics of the media today and their inter-
connections with political life, to call our time the Age of Personality is almost an understatement. And, with advanced communications technology on a global scale, the ancient metaphor
of "the world stage" takes on a new and more compelling meaning. Mikhail Gorbachev is as much a creature of the Age of Personality as any American public figure.

The essays that follow explore several different provinces of our political world. They wander here and there and all about, but probing the relationship between statecraft and stagecraft — for now and for the future — will serve as the compass and point the way.

1

Smokeless Politics

Political and cultural seismologists continue to measure the after-shocks of the year-long earthquake that convulsed America in 1968. Event collided with event, affecting that time and changing the future. The then-popular chant of discontented youth, "The whole world is watching," was actually a statement of fact. The media, especially television, served as the prisms through which these events unfolded. The words and pictures remain vivid.

To mention in chronological sequence some of the significant occurrences:

- In the wake of the bloody and controversial Tet offensive in Vietnam, President Lyndon Johnson wins the New Hampshire presidential primary of the Democratic Party, but unexpectedly defeats an anti-war senator, Eugene Mc-Carthy, only 48.5 percent to 42 percent.
- Nineteen days later and with Senator Robert Kennedy having announced his candidacy for the Democratic presidential nomination, Johnson declares he will not seek re-election.
- Civil rights leader Martin Luther King, Jr., is fatally shot in Memphis.
- Victorious in the California primary, Robert Kennedy is assassinated in Los Angeles the night of the triumph.
- Former Vice President Richard Nixon receives the Republican presidential nomination and surprises the nation by

1

selecting an obscure governor from a small state, Spiro Agnew of Maryland, as his running mate.

- Without campaigning in any primaries and amid what was subsequently called a "police riot" at the Democratic Convention in Chicago, incumbent Vice President Hubert Humphrey captures his party's presidential nomination.
- Nixon defeats Humphrey by collecting 43.4 percent to 42.7 percent of the total vote. Third-party candidate George Wallace takes 13.5 percent.

Without the election of Richard Nixon the word "Watergate" would be meaningful to only the relatively few people who have seen this oddly designed Washington building. Without Robert Kennedy the Democratic Party had no compelling figure to unite its diverse constituencies — the young and the old, the black and the white, the blue collar and the white collar. Without Martin Luther King, Jr., black America had no commanding voice or rallying human symbol until the emergence of Jesse Jackson in the 1980s.

Far-reaching consequences, for people and for institutions, continue to reverberate as a result of the events of 1968. These events removed certain public figures from American political life and replaced them with others. What happened also triggered fundamental structural changes within our political system. These changes dramatically altered the relationship between public life and popular communication, leading to the current interplay between statecraft and stagecraft.

Throughout the spring and summer of 1968, Democrats opposed to the presidential nomination of Vice President Hubert Humphrey criticized his failure to get involved in the primaries. Seemingly without doing battle, the Happy Warrior was on his way to victory. Questions about democratic fairness and the value of primaries arose. Just before the bloody days of the Chicago convention, a commission headed by Governor Harold Hughes of Iowa (personally sympathetic to the candidacy of McCarthy) released a report, *The Democratic Choice*, detailing abuses in the selection process. Noting that "state systems for selecting delegates to the national convention and the procedures of the con-

vention itself, display considerably less fidelity to basic democratic principles than a nation which claims to govern itself can
safely tolerate," the report called for a formal commission of the
Democratic Party to investigate its rules and procedures.

In early 1969, the Commission on Party Structure and Delegate Selection came into being, led by Senator George McGovern. To a considerable extent the work of this commission is responsible for the political reformation that has been taking place
in America during the past twenty years. In the guidelines it produced, the McGovern Commission repeatedly emphasized the
necessity of opening up the delegate selection process. Political
bargaining behind closed doors would no longer have as much
clout as it had previously enjoyed. As one paragraph of the guidelines states, "The 1968 Convention indicated no preference between primary, convention, and committee systems for choosing
delegates. The Commission believes, however, that committee
systems by virtue of their indirect relationship to the delegate
selection process, offer fewer guarantees for a full and meaningful opportunity to participate than other systems." The Republican party has not instituted as many reforms as the Democrats
since the late 1960s, but among other changes the GOP has more
than doubled its number of presidential primaries.

Creating a more open, participatory system produced significant consequences, both symbolically and substantively. Gone
were the days of the smoke-filled room where party officials (con-
noisseurs of large cigars, according to the stereotype) privately
debated the strengths and weaknesses of prospective candidates
before deciding which ones had the best chances of winning the
election and governing effectively. The pre-1968 primaries were
little more than tryouts to see whether someone had the requi-
site "fire in the belly" and resources to mount a full-scale fall production. The new era of smokeless politics would throw open the
doors of democracy, even on the candidate selection level, to larger
numbers of party members. The same doors would also be open
to members of the media who had more political action to cover
— without smoke getting in their eyes or on their camera lenses.

The proliferation of primaries in both the Democratic and Republican parties is one dimension of this new era. In 1968 there
were fifteen primaries in each party, yielding about one-third
of the candidate-committed delegates to the conventions. The

numbers fluctuate from year to year, but today nearly forty states conduct primaries, producing about 75 percent of committed delegates. More primaries mean more direct appeals by candidates to voters. Hence, at the nominating stage, these candidates need not pay much attention to having the party organizations serve as intermediaries between themselves and the public.

With the party structure less significant, the popular forms of communication have become the critical link between the candidates and citizens. Coached by communications consultants and guided by public opinion pollsters — conspicuous political participants since the post-1968 reformation — candidates rely on ads, press conferences, photo opportunities and myriad other media-related events to deliver their messages. Smokeless politics makes the various modes of mass communication, especially television, central participants in the electoral process. It is largely through the media that we come to know and to judge public figures. A campaign becomes a political production that dramatizes and projects the candidate's personality as well as his policies and proposals.

Buying advertising time and space allows a political figure his or her say. The media deliver the message, whether it be uplifting or eye-gouging. At the same time, the journalistic sides of the media organizations offer their own messages in the form of campaign reports, which may or may not be consistent with what the candidate presents. As a result, newspapers, magazines, television, and radio now serve as an unofficial — yet influential — "check" in assessing whatever the candidate says and does. Journalists ask: Are the statements and images credible or contrived? Do other facts or circumstances shed light on a public figure's potential performance? The role of journalism in contemporary American politics is vastly different today from what it was in 1968 because the electoral system itself has changed. The media — both as advertisers and as news reporters — really *mediate* between a candidate and the citizenry. The joke that nowadays a political rally consists of three people watching a television commercial in their living rooms is more telling than funny.

The decline of party dominance and discipline has opened the selection process and placed much greater focus on the individual candidate. A distinctly American cult of the personality has replaced meaningful party allegiance. In general elections ticket-splitting is now customary. Getting on the November ballot means mobilizing a core constituency of support. Just as today's communication on radio and television is more accurately called narrowcasting instead of broadcasting, our politics has narrowed, promoting single-minded and personality-driven factions rather than the more collegial coalitions of common purpose that the parties strived to achieve in earlier days. This fragmenting of our politics endangers the bonding spirit of pluralism that in earlier times symbolically, if not substantively, served to unify the nation.

The dangers of factionalism have long been recognized in American political life. In *The Federalists Papers* (Number 10), James Madison discusses "the mischiefs of faction" and offers proposals "to break and control the violence of faction." However, the nominating system that currently exists gives factions, particularly in the form of special interest groups, considerable power in determining party nominees. The Iowa caucus and the New Hampshire primary are now highly visible and important, although neither state is large nor demographically representative. In both cases and in other similar circumstances, a candidate can target appeals to a relatively small yet faithful group and reap significant rewards — such as more media attention and the perception of viability that leads to contributions.

For the Democrats the beneficiaries of the post-1968 party rules to select presidential candidates have been George McGovern, Jimmy Carter, Walter Mondale, and Michael Dukakis. Each nominee effectively manipulated the party regulations with their emphasis on primaries. However, instead of building coalitions that would enhance their performances in the general election and (in the singular case of Carter) in the White House, the four tended to rely on relatively small factions to secure their positions against the multitude of candidates running in the primaries.

In *Consequences of Party Reform*, the political scientist Nelson Polsby argues that the good intentions of constructing a more participatory system have led to questionable results. He writes,

> Why must a presidential candidate in the new circumstances created by the proliferation of primaries mobilize his faction rather than build coalitions? The task of a presidential hopeful, threading a path through the minefield of successive primary elections, is not to win a majority but rather to survive. Survival means gaining as high as possible a rank among the candidates running for election. Coming in first in early pri-

maries means achieving the visibility that ensures that a candidate will be taken seriously by the news media.[1]

Since the reforms were promulgated, the Democrats—leaders in party identification in all but a handful of studies since survey research in the 1930s began to measure political allegiance—have lost four of five presidential elections, with Carter victorious in 1976 by just 2 percent. In that same period, voter independence has been conspicuous. On the federal electoral level, the Democrats have never relinquished control of the House of Representatives, while the Republicans had a majority in the Senate for six years, from 1981 until 1987.

The closeness of the 1968 election (a half-million votes, 0.7 percent dividing Nixon and Humphrey) gave rise to analytical speculation about the reasons behind the victory and the defeat. Was it—positively for Nixon—a desire to change the direction of government away from the policies that produced the Great Society and the Vietnam War? Was it—negatively for Humphrey —a time of such division among Democrats (supporters of Mc-Carthy and Kennedy remained bruised in the aftermath of the Chicago convention) that it was not possible to collect enough votes of party members and independents?

The Nixon campaign that year masterfully exploited television. Eight years earlier, when he lost by a mere 100,000 votes to John Kennedy, the Nixon of the then-novel televised debates looked like (in the phrase of Marshall McLuhan) "the railway lawyer who signs leases that are not in the interests of the folks in the little town." In *The Making of the President 1960*, Theodore White quotes Kennedy as saying: "It was TV more than anything that turned the tide." By contrast, the dustjacket of Joe McGinniss's *The Selling of the President 1968* features this statement of Humphrey: "The biggest mistake in my political life was not to learn how to use television." Although politicians are notorious for saying outrageously foolish things about television, these remarks, tested against history, have the ring of credibility.

Nixon had learned the lesson that statecraft and stagecraft go hand-in-hand. However, this "new Nixon" with the more appealing personality was really a facade. Behind the mask lived the calculating, sometimes cruel "old Nixon," whose personal agenda to secure and wield power, *his way*, could not remain hidden for too long.

The "third-rate burglary" of Democratic Party offices at the Watergate Hotel in June 1972 started an avalanche. What Gerald Ford called "our long national nightmare" (the most memorable utterance of his presidency) had profound consequences in our political life, possibly the least important being the resignation of a president. The machinations of Nixon supporters in the election of 1972 ultimately led to the enactment of the Federal Election Campaign Act Amendments of 1974. This legislation created such provisions as federal funding of presidential elections, nominating conventions, and much of the primary campaigning; limits on expenditures by candidates accepting federal financing; restrictions on the amounts of money individuals can give to candidates, and strict reporting of contributions to and expenditures by candidates.

These regulations, which like the party reforms were conceived with worthy intentions, have themselves spawned problems for both of the major parties. For example, candidates and their campaign officials are much more inclined to direct their limited funds to advertising through the media, especially television, rather than to the grass roots of door-to-door political activity. The personal dimension of "retail politics" becomes subordinate to mediated messages of "wholesale politics." Moreover, a candidate needs to invest a sizeable amount of time raising the required matching contributions, state-by-state, and an army of accountants has to keep track of the money coming in and going out.

Rules dictate how a candidate runs. Radically different rules markedly change the course, leading to a different kind of politics and to the possibility of a different type of participant. Enlarging the involvement of popular modes of communication has, among other things, fostered candidates (such as Jimmy Carter and George Bush) who emphasize their images over ideas about issues and substantially reduced the intermediary function of the political parties.

T he environment of our contemporary political life is, in large measure, shaped by actions and attitudes that have their roots in the bloody soil of 1968. The formal party and election reforms, along with the informal yet dominant role now played by popular communication, create a new process. As Polsby remarks in *Consequences of Party Reform*, "The 'old' rules were 'old' poli-

tics. 'New politics' demanded new and more democratic rules."
The new process along with the new politics are offspring of
virtuous intentions. Conceptually, there is a Fourth of July Amer-
icanism to a system that emphasizes both broad citizen participation and a watchdog agency (such as the Federal Election
Commission) to monitor where political money goes. Practically,
however, it is legitimate to wonder about the actual effects of
these new rules and requirements on our political culture and
public life.

Anyone who spends any time studying and thinking about the
design of our governmental system comes away with admiring
regard for its logic, balance, consistency, and fairness. Despite
noisy and seemingly endless debates over matters affecting the
body politic, the three branches share power and authority in
an understandable way. (Beyond the Potomac River, the states,
too, have similar governmental structures, with federalism linking the national and state governments.) There is a coherence
and rationality to our separate-but-equal system that is easily
grasped by an elementary student.

That same student would, no doubt, have a different opinion
of the electoral process that produces the candidates who vie to
lead the executive branch and to appoint judges to life-time terms
on the federal judiciary. This post-1968 process is so complex and
illogical that it defies comprehension by most citizens. It is as
though the original design was done by cartoonist Rube Gold-
berg, with subsequent modifications suggested by Erno Rubik,
of Rubik's Cube renown. The machine — or puzzle — yields results.
But the type of results and how we get those results should make
us pause.

Viewed objectively, the complicated process of nomination
lacks the structural orderliness of the American governmental
system. There is so much variation among the individual states
and so many changes from year to year (for example, discussions
continue about moving the California primary from June to early
March, just after New Hampshire, giving California more clout)
that the process itself creates a barrier between the public and
their political life. The Iowa caucus, the New Hampshire primary, and the variety of political experiences that make up "Super
Tuesday" offer diverse campaign challenges — but not necessarily reasonable ones. Why do Iowa and New Hampshire enjoy the

early advantage? Why make so much of anything-but-secret balloting in Iowa that brings out true believers but diminishes the role of the rank-and-file party members? Why should one region, the South, try to toss its collective elbows at the rest of the country for the sake of a common influence on the eventual selection of presidential candidates?

Residents in these states have definite justifications for the existing system. They say states have certain rights, and they express themselves with a pluralistic individualism that caters to our indigenous suspicion of power. In addition, the early results *count* more heavily — not only in sending candidates to the front of the race but in ending the competition of others — and the states involved can take pride in being so influential.

But citizens in other states frequently have a different view of this electoral maze. Despite the massive media coverage of, say, the Iowa caucus, what is actually happening is confusing at best and inscrutable at worst. Popular communication is in the business of simplification. Try as they might, the different forms of communication cannot do justice to the complexity of the step-by-step delegate-selection process that the Iowa caucus initiates — let alone the vagaries of the specific rules that apply in each of the other forty-nine states.

The media, with an eye to a national audience, can transmit what occurs along the campaign gauntlet, and coverage of debates, forums, and speeches are valuable in the get-acquainted stage of the process. However, with the system so complex, the media focus on the actors involved. This approach personalizes the process, making much of winners and losers. In 1976, 37 percent of the Iowa caucus vote was uncommitted. Jimmy Carter received 27 percent, and became by virtue of his showing the frontrunner. Momentum from this performance (fewer than 14,000 Iowans voted for Carter) and his showing in the New Hampshire primary (again less than 30 percent of the total) constructed a bandwagon that ultimately helped carry the one-term Georgia governor to the nomination and eventually to the White House. He, conveniently, spent the night of the Iowa caucus in New York so that the next morning he could appear on ABC, CBS, and NBC.

The media contribute substantially to our political environment, but as much as anything they amplify what is taking place within boundaries established by those responsible for designing the system. Journalists focus on Iowa and New Hampshire because they, formally, are the first events in the nomination marathon. That the media overly magnify the significance of these two states is a problem of proportion rather than news definition. Because of the hype surrounding the Iowa caucus it seems more like the final game of the World Series instead of Opening Day. However, given the public's shortening attention span and the similar media-conditioned phenomenon of subject fatigue — a topic will hold our interest for a limited time before we feel saturated and become bored — the coverage of the earliest contests is critical in setting a tone.

A citizen watching the process unfold is perplexed, but there is another reaction, too. The citizen has the disquieting feeling that the existing system is unfair. Who says certain states should have political priority? Why do some of us have fewer choices to consider than folks who decide sooner? Shouldn't candidates for the highest national office be selected following a more methodical national plan?

Is it too unrealistic to ask that the electoral system on the presidential level reflect some of the characteristics of our governmental system — the logic, balance, consistency, and fairness? Given the centrality of the presidency in influencing the totality of our political life, a new — and improved — selection system could produce a trickle-down effect, stimulating participation for other offices and greater interest in public life in general.

Although they've been treated like clay pigeons thus far, proposals to revamp the current process exist in abundance. Political scientists, journalists, and public officials have suggested everything from abolishing primaries altogether to establishing one national primary to creating a sequence of regional primaries. One plan advocates a national caucus or convention of elected officials and party leaders that would choose a certain number of candidates for a national primary ballot. This proposal emphasizes peer review — people in government and politics decide who they think can win election and competently govern — but it has the aroma of cigar smoke. Even if the caucus or convention were conducted in full public view of the media, there would be a perception that "insiders" were calling the shots. Given the current environment of smokeless politics and the enlarging of democratic involvement that marks our history, it is difficult to imagine acceptance of such a plan. Perception is frequently as influential as reality.

A series of regional primaries, however, would stress an open process for party members in all of the states. One proposal, advocated by some members of Congress, establishes six regional primaries to be conducted two weeks apart from the end of March through part of June. Each region would include eight or nine contiguous states, with the order of participation determined by lot. (A variation of this proposal, which emphasizes candidate-with-people "retail" politics, puts two or three individual states, again picked randomly, ahead of the regional contests.)

The regional primary approach has several advantages. The system fosters open participation in a system that is understandable to the people at large. Gone would be the extreme of an Iowa caucus that is followed a month later by so-called "Super Tuesday" with some twenty states involved, as happened in 1988. No state or region would receive systemic preferential treatment, because potential candidates would not know where to campaign until lots were drawn in the November or December of the year preceding a presidential election. A shorter nominating season would also offer a more sharply focused contest, resulting in less boredom or subject fatigue by the public. It also might be a deciding factor in the minds of potential candidates, who are not inclined to invest substantial amounts of time trekking around Iowa or New Hampshire a year or more before the caucus and primary.

National legislation is the only remedy. Among other advantages, a more comprehensible process reduces the potential of factionalism. Having so many narrow, single-interest groups leads candidates to the political fringes in the winter only to have the two nominees race for the center in the fall. A reinvigorated role for the parties is another benefit of a more coherent procedure. More understanding promotes more participation at this party level. More vigorous party structures reduce public reliance on the different forms of popular communication as intermediaries between the people and their public life, governmental and electoral.

In addition, a more accessible nominating system gives the media greater opportunity to offer their coverage with clarity and proportion. The often-criticized horse-race characteristics of today's campaign reporting would not immediately disappear — nor should they. In the United States candidates definitely *run* for office, and the public needs to know who is ahead, who is behind, and why. Instead of devoting space and time to explanations of the mysteries of this caucus or that cross-over primary, the media could work to strike a balance in reporting about both the program and personality of the candidates. There might even be less absorption in stories about campaign strategies and tactics as well as diminished reliance on polls, which do little to offer civic nourishment.

It is easy for the purveyors of personality to become overly absorbed in individual matters of small moment and even smaller political consequence. Candidate debates have become increasingly trivialized, as the reporting, analysis, and commentary revolves around assigning a clear victor or assessing image-oriented concerns such as appearance and style of delivery. Following each debate in 1988 (two between Bush and Dukakis and one between Dan Quayle and Lloyd Bentsen), the networks seemed to take delight in what they called "spin patrol." These utterly predictable encounters between journalists and campaign workers focused on the supporters spouting definite — if not defensible — reasons their candidate was convincingly triumphant. Probing in greater depth what was actually said during a debate would be a more valuable use of everyone's time.

The road to a more orderly and equitable nominating system is not an easy one. Entrenched self-interests of individual states and specific regions are formidable barriers. A public figure with even a faint desire to seek the presidency — which, one guesses, includes most members of Congress, a high percentage of governors, and several mayors — is reluctant to become a political pariah in, say, Iowa or New Hampshire. Talk of procedural change captures attention during chaotic moments of a campaign year, but seems to get lost in the legislative shuffle after the inauguration. Even a presidential contest between "the evil of two lessers," as someone dubbed the much-criticized 1988 election campaign, quickly becomes a distant memory without providing impetus for needed reform.

As the ground shifted and cracked in 1968, the direction of any road to a political future was largely determined. In addition, the system itself was opened up, a phenomenon that prevents any serious consideration of a return to decisions coming from smoke-filled rooms. As an Iowa farmer told *Time* before his state's caucus, "I can't stand cigar smoke. I believe in democracy. It's a duty." For better or worse, the era of smokeless politics is here to stay, contributing atmospherically and substantively to whatever might take place in our future political life. For the citizenry at large, though, the real duty now is the design of a more coherent electoral system that fosters effective statecraft.

2

Image-Making and
Anti-Image Journalism

While filming the television version of his memoirs in 1971, Lyndon Johnson and a CBS producer were casually talking about the former president's experiences when the producer asked about changes in political life during the previous thirty years. The question struck a nerve, abruptly changing the mood. According to David Halberstam, who tells the story in *The Powers That Be*, Johnson flared: "You guys. All you guys in the media. All of politics has changed because of you. You've broken all the machines and the ties between us in Congress and the city machines. You've given us a new kind of people."

The new political breed that Johnson referred to began to emerge in the 1960s and multiplied rapidly in the following two decades. This "new kind of people" did not foster strong links to party organizations, contributing to a decline in the parties themselves. They exploited other ways of establishing connections to the public at large. An expanding media environment allowed these political figures to base much of their relationship with the citizenry on mediated messages delivered by popular forms of communication. The post-1960s politicians quickly learned that emphasizing image and personality helped to define themselves in the public mind.

It is not an accident that the Age of Personality coincides with the growth of television as the primary source of news for most

Americans. In major political races, television — essentially a medium that projects personality — is the single greatest beneficiary of a candidate's campaign resources. The so-called "free media" of journalistic coverage and the "paid media" of advertising join together in forming the mediated bond between the public figure and the public.

The penchant for cultivating a favorable impression is, of course, not something new. In his autobiography Benjamin Franklin confesses to studied self-dramatization:

> In order to secure my credit and character as a tradesman, I took care not only to be in *reality* industrious and frugal, but to avoid all appearances to the contrary. I never went out a fishing or shooting; a book, indeed, sometimes debauch'd me from my work, but that was seldom, snug, and gave no scandal; and, to show that I was not above my business, I sometimes brought home the paper I purchase'd at the stores thro' the streets on a wheelbarrow.

In the political realm, the presidential campaign in 1840 between Martin Van Buren and William Henry Harrison is a case study of image-oriented artifice. Attempting to put an end to twelve years of Jacksonian rule — Van Buren had served as Andrew Jackson's vice president and had been elected in 1836 after Jackson's two terms — the Whigs presented Harrison with qualities at considerable variance with reality. The affluent descendant of Virginia aristocracy with a distinguished military record, Harrison was reborn politically as the product of a log cabin and with a fondness for hard cider. The Whigs offered no platform that year, and Harrison avoided any statements of substance. The songs, symbols, and slogans ("Tippecanoe and Tyler, too") made up the entire campaign, with the fiction and myth being appealing enough for victory.

The historian Daniel Boorstin performed a national service by writing *The Image*, published in 1962. By explaining the phenomena of celebrity, pseudo-events, round-the-clock media, dissolving forms, and extravagant expectations, he exposed the twentieth-century American's obsession with grand illusions. As he repeatedly points out, the popular modes of mass communication are principally responsible for shaping this environment of shadows over shapes, of the superficial over the substantial.

Boorstin describes the extent to which Americans have become entranced by superficial appearances, especially those transmitted through the mass media. His analysis even influenced the nation's vocabulary. A celebrity *is* a "human pseudo-event," someone "who is known for his well-knownness." His word "image" itself has in recent years become omnipresent, if not terribly illuminating, in discussions of various aspects of American life. Some historians, in fact, engage in catch-phrase revisionism, now calling the election of 1840 "The Image Campaign" rather than its time-honored nickname, "The Log-Cabin Campaign."

Although the preoccupation with image is a consequence of the rise of television and of the dominant role of advertising and public relations in the United States after World War II, there are certain parallels between the relatively recent concern for image and the more academically rooted concept of *persona*. Throughout this century, literary critics and psychologists have often wrestled with interpreting the similarities and differences between the mask or alter-ego of someone, on one hand, and that same person's private self, on the other. For example, recent studies of the work of Mark Twain often focus on the relationship between the life of Samuel Clemens and the dramatized, first-person rendering of the pseudonymous creation, Mark Twain.

In *Two Essays on Analytical Psychology*, Carl Jung notes: "The persona is a complicated system of relations between the individual consciousness and society, fittingly enough a kind of mask, designed on the one hand to make a definite impression upon others, and, on the other, to conceal the true nature of the individual." On the surface, image is not all that different from persona. William Safire in *Safire's Political Dictionary* defines image as "the impression of himself that a public figure attempts to convey; the merchandising of reputation." Later in the entry, however, Safire says, "Many politicians misuse the word to mean something that belongs to them, much as Peter Pan's shadow, and feel lost without it; the fact is that an image belongs to the public."[1]

While persona has inner direction and emphasis, an image has greater outer direction and effect. How an image is interpreted and received is critical. Frequently the product of instruments of popular communication, an image involves both conscious self-dramatization *and* public perception. The case of George Bush is illustrative. From his ill-fated 1980 campaign for the Republican presidential nomination through his eight years as vice president, an image of ineffectual weakness dogged his steps, creating public uneasiness about his ability to be a strong leader. In the cartoon "Doonesbury" Garry Trudeau wondered about a blind trust for Bush's manhood. A cover story in *Newsweek* a year before the 1988 election was headlined "Bush Battles the 'Wimp Factor'."

Changing that image, that perception of personality, became an overriding concern of his strategy throughout the campaign of 1988. A calculatingly combative Bush took on Dan Rather for nine minutes of live television on the "CBS Evening News" in late January 1988, a few weeks before the Iowa caucus. Although it did not save him from a poor third-place finish in Iowa, the encounter was the first volley in a continuing struggle to change Bush's image. (That he did not answer questions about his own role in the Iran-*contra* imbroglio was of secondary importance to scrappily going toe-to-toe with a journalistic heavyweight.) Bush subsequently talked tough about dealing with criminals, and would not go as far as Ronald Reagan in supporting measures to reduce tensions between the United States and the Soviet Union. His repeated use of the flag, too, symbolically represented a strong appeal to patriotism and fighting for our nation's future. During the campaign against Michael Dukakis, Bush was largely successful in altering the public's perception of himself. It pays to advertise—and to hire advertisers as consultants.

Few post-mortems of the 1988 campaign fail to note that Bush's image consultant, Roger Ailes, served in a similar capacity for Richard Nixon in 1968. Ailes, in fact, figures prominently in *The Selling of the President 1968* by Joe McGinniss. In describing the conflict between old style and new style politics, McGinniss notes that, instead of being a welcome guest in our homes, Hubert Humphrey "vomited on the rug" by coming on too strong on the intimate medium of television. With coaching from Ailes, Nixon was different, and using the media effectively proved critical in cultivating a favorable, vote-triggering impression.

In the appendix to his book, McGinniss publishes several in-

ternal memoranda by people who worked on the Nixon campaign. A 1967 memo by Ray Price, one of the members of the
communications team, dramatizes the concern for image that
pervaded the Nixon election effort. Using italics to emphasize his
points, Price wrote:

> *We have to be very clear on this point: that the response is
> to the image, not to the man,* since 99 percent of the voters
> have no contact with the man. It's not what's *there* that counts,
> it's what's projected — and, carrying it one step further, it's not
> what *he* projects but rather what the voter receives. It's not
> the man we have to change, but rather the *received impres-
> sion.* And this impression often depends more on the medium
> and its use than it does on the candidate himself.[2]

The unnamed medium is, of course, television, an instrument of
almost obsessive concern to Nixon's campaign staff and to those
who served him in the White House from 1969 until 1974. The
1968 campaign would not be lost on television screens as they believed the close 1960 election had been — a study by survey re-
searcher Elmo Roper revealed that 2,000,000 people chose John
Kennedy primarily because of his performance in the televised
debates.

Benefiting from better make-up and professional stage direction, the Nixon of 1968 projected experience, intellectual ability,
acceptability, integrity, conscientiousness, firmness, warmth, and,
yes, even humor. In short, again to use words from Price's memo,
the public was provided with "a *received* image of RN as the kind
of man proud parents would ideally want their sons to grow up
to be: a man who embodies the national ideal, its aspirations,
its dreams, a man whose *image* the people want in their homes
as a source of inspiration, and whose voice they want as the representative of their nation in the councils of the world, and of
their generation in the pages of history."[3] (Looking back with
post-Watergate hindsight, it is difficult not to laugh, or at least
knowingly smirk, at these statements.) However, the strategic
effort in 1968 — effective image-making and image-projection
through controlled use of television — worked. This, of course,
was the same man who had retired from politics in 1962 after
losing the California governor's race and becoming angry at the
media for kicking him around. Now, successful stagecraft helped
give Nixon a new life to perform statecraft.

By contrast, core concerns of image-usage seemed lost on Jimmy Carter, hampering him in his 1976 campaign and throughout much of his four years as president. Candidate Carter, with his telegenic smile and his one-of-us gesture of carrying his garment bag on and off airplanes, as well as President Carter, with his Inauguration Day walk down Pennsylvania Avenue and his cardigan sweater for a Fireside chat, revealed an acute understanding of television's image-making influence and its inherent quality of communicating visually through symbols. During the 1976 campaign, however, this realization did *not* translate into skillful projection of a coherent and appealing image. He tried too hard to offer something to everyone. The first chapter of his autobiography *Why Not the Best?* includes this remarkable passage: "I am a Southerner and an American. I am a farmer, an engineer, a father and husband, a Christian, a politician and former governor, a planner, a businessman, a nuclear physicist, a naval officer, a canoeist, and among other things, a lover of Bob Dylan's songs and Dylan Thomas' poetry."

Upon entering the quest for the Democratic nomination — something he began with full knowledge of both the post-1968 rules and the amplifying power of television — the virtually unknown Carter quite consciously tried to identify with several, almost contradictory constituencies. During the primary and caucus season, he came across as an economic moderate or conservative, as an outsider to Democratic Party machine politics, and as a devoutly religious man with words of compassion and love for everyone.

In the fall of 1976, however, he began his general campaign in Warm Springs, Georgia, by tracing his lineage to the economic liberalism of frequent Warm Springs visitor Franklin Roosevelt. He then went to Chicago and Philadelphia to embrace party-cum-machine bosses Richard J. Daley and Frank Rizzo. He confessed to *Playboy* a modicum of covetous lust in his heart. After the second debate with President (and Republican candidate) Gerald Ford, which included Ford's gaffe about Poland being free of Soviet domination, Carter intemperately said the president had been "brainwashed" and that the statement was a "disgrace." These actions and words of the autumn stood in stark juxtaposition to what we had learned about him in the winter and spring. Carter got caught in a crossfire of conflicting images. A puzzled public did not know how to interpret the very different images that the media, principally television, transmitted.

The beneficiary of the doubt was, of course, Ford. Although hampered by lingering public resentment to his pardon of Nixon and a general feeling of the need to fumigate the White House after the blight of Watergate, Ford effectively stressed the image of the incumbent chief executive at work through a Rose Garden strategy. Carter's lead dropped from a commanding fifteen-point advantage just after Labor Day to a 2 percent margin of victory. In the minds of many people, Carter was not so much "fuzzy on the issues," a popular charge at the time, as he was fuzzy as a person. The projected image did not remain consistent or coherent, a problem that also plagued his presidency and contributed to his defeat by Ronald Reagan in 1980. Despite misstatements of fact and a self-admitted reluctance to work overtime on public matters, the former governor of California was a known commodity with a definite, established image in America's public mind. He proposed different policies *and* a different style of leadership. With the inconsistent image of Carter converging with economic problems and the Iranian hostage crisis, Reagan won convincingly. His victory ushered to the fore a reliance on stagecraft in statecraft. This reliance, however, coexisted with other elements in the political-media environment.

T he long-playing record of Watergate, with one bizarre revelation following another, was the catalyst to the boom in election reforms and, less formally but importantly, in political ethics. How public officials conducted themselves became a subject of intense concern, especially among journalists. The work of Carl Bernstein, Bob Woodward, and others who covered the Watergate saga also helped create a new ethos in American journalism. A growing skepticism pervaded the reporting about the Vietnam War. What all the president's men wrought turned this skepticism into suspicion.

The establishment-challenging reporter assumed heroic status in American popular culture. Trench coats sold briskly. Enrollment in collegiate journalism programs exploded. Most critically, the investigative spirit of not just covering but *uncovering* a story took hold, influencing in varying ways the different modes and kinds of popular communication.

A small but enduring legacy of the post-Watergate journalistic ethos is the frequent use of the suffix "-gate" in reports that raise any suspicion of scandal. Since Nixon's resignation in 1974, the news media have covered "Koreagate" (the gifts-for-favors affair involving members of Congress and Korean lobbyist Tongsun Park), "Lancegate" (questionable financial dealings of Carter administration official Bert Lance), "Billygate" (Billy Carter's alleged influence-peddling with Libya), "Hollywoodgate" (the embezzling of money by a prominent studio mogul), "Debategate" (the pilfering of Jimmy Carter's briefing book by supporters of Ronald Reagan before a debate in 1980), "Ponygate" (the transgressions with the football program of the Mustangs of Southern Methodist University), and, of course, "Irangate" or "Iran-Contragate" (the folly of the Reagan administration to sell arms to Iran with profits going to support the Contras in Nicaragua). This list is highly selective and does not include instances of the widespread local usage or the contrived attempts of being clever. The *New York Times* referred to "Debategate" as "Pseudo-Gate" in one follow-up story, while a network sports announcer called the SMU scandal "Ponytailgate," when charges of involvement of women students in recruiting began to surface.

This kind of media shorthand simplifies communication about complicated subjects and gives aid and comfort to our stereotypes. With "-gateism," however, the affixing of the suffix on a convenient word makes us consider wrongdoing or suspected wrongdoing as being similar to what happened during the Watergate affair. Such stereotyping trivializes a significant historical experience by making it an all-purpose point of reference. In addition, the practice — as common today as in the mid-1970s — subtly yet consciously reveals a nostalgia for the big story by some people in journalism. The romance of becoming the next Woodward or Bernstein is still alive, making news people more aggressive in pursuing figures in the public eye. Former presidential press secretary and now journalist Bill Moyers calls this phenomenon "the Woodward-Bernstein factor." He goes on to say: "If on earth's last lonely road a single stone is left unturned, two reporters will bump their heads kneeling down trying to be the first to turn it over."

The emphasis on image-projection and image-reception, so prevalent in American political life from the 1960s on, has other consequences. People want to know what a political figure stands for, but increasingly they also desire information about what the figure is "really like." The phrase "really like" suggests a general, unarticulated understanding that what we see as the public image has elements of construction or concealment. Finding out the extent to which the image conforms to reality becomes a matter of no small interest. What kind — and how many — clothes does a democratic emperor wear?

A proliferation of personality journalism began to appear in print and broadcast media during the mid-1970s. At the time, the conventional explanation for such journalism was that the public felt overwhelmed by the issues and events of the 1960s and early 1970s. Racial conflict, assassinations, the Vietnam war, and Watergate had exhausted the citizenry. People wanted to get off the roller coaster of momentous national events and turn at least some of their attention to less intellectually demanding news subjects — namely the personalities or celebrities of our culture. The success of *People*, which first appeared in 1974 shortly before Nixon resigned, underscores the popular appeal of this type of journalism. As the magazine's editor emphatically announced with the première issue, "Our focus is on people, not issues." The circulation of *People*, originally at 1.4 million copies, now stands at over 3 million, with, of course, a much larger readership.

In 1922 in *Public Opinion*, Walter Lippmann surveyed newspapers and magazines of post–World War I America and noted a "preference for the curious trivial as against the dull important, and the hunger for sideshows and three legged calves." Nowadays, what Lippmann termed a "preference" and "hunger" might be more appropriately called an obsession, with personalities or celebrities cornering much of "the curious trivial" market. A trend became a growth industry, with numerous subsidiaries in the public prints and on the airwaves.

Book publishing is a conspicuous example. An exposé of the famous — dead and living — has a fairly certain route to the bestseller list. Reviewing one biography of a celebrated writer, Joyce Carol Oates coined a new term to classify the genre it represented: "pathography." There are also "kiss-and-tell" or "tell-all" memoirs and "insider" or "secret life" accounts — all with the objective of going behind the scenes to chronicle more private matters. In the political realm, David Stockman, Michael Deaver, Donald Regan, Larry Speakes, and others had published books about everything from the fabrication of presidential statements at a summit meeting with Mikhail Gorbachev to Oval Office scheduling in consultation with an astrologer before Reagan had left office.

Such books are part of today's political culture, which, of course, exists within the broader national culture. The same type of exposure is given to all recipients of public attention or fame, for example, Elizabeth Taylor, or Jackie Kennedy Onassis. This boom in personality journalism took place as people in the news media operated under the influence of the heady experience of playing a role in the decline and fall of a president. Communications cross-pollination yielded an acute interest in personality and a let's-know-everything inquisitiveness about subjects. Stories with these characteristics appear now as a matter of course in coverage of entertainment, sports, business, science, the law, and political life.

In *The Image*, Boorstin asserts, "Strictly speaking, there is no way to unmask an image." The communications environment has changed so profoundly in the past two decades, this observation is now obsolete. Today, much that we read or see reported could be called anti-image journalism. News people are probing behind the projected images to see whether there might be inconsistencies or discrepancies between what someone (or some institution) presents and the reality of the situation. This anti-image attitude now pervades the coverage of public affairs, redefining the relationship between reporters and public figures. It used to be accepted practice for journalists to avoid treatment of an official's or candidate's private life unless there was significant public relevance to the personal disclosure. Those making news judgments thought it was none of our business that, say, John Kennedy's roving eye led to presidential promiscuity. That was then. Today almost any area of a public figure's existence — present and past — is open for scrutiny.

The experiences of some of the people contending for the Democratic and Republican nominations for president in 1988 underline the extent to which anti-image journalism operates today. In May 1987, the *Miami Herald* conducted surveillance of Gary Hart's townhouse in Washington, D.C., and reported the former Colorado senator was entertaining a young woman for the weekend, while his wife was 1,600 miles away at their home near Denver. This disclosure, which gave birth to celebrity status for the young woman (Donna Rice) and to countless jokes of dubious taste, came at a time when Hart, the clear leader for the nomination, was publicly asserting the stability of his marriage. In fact, on the very day when the *Miami Herald* revealed the results of its flawed and professionally questionable stake-out, the cover story of the *New York Times Magazine* focused on "the elusive front-runner," with Hart quoted as saying, "Follow me around. I don't care. I'm serious. If anybody wants to put a tail on me, go ahead. They'd be very bored." Hart's monkey business (so named for the boat Hart and Rice had taken to Bimini during an earlier tryst) was anything but boring. Journalistic outlets for every brow, high to low, became absorbed in covering the story. *People* and the supermarket tabloids had a field day, pronouncing the former model a "Hart Stopper," which she, in effect, was. Hart withdrew from the race, returning several months later in a farcical attempt at personal and political rehabilitation.

The damage was done. Despite substantial, detailed knowledge of public policy matters and the publication of paper after paper that put flesh on his "new ideas," Hart could not be taken seriously because what he projected as part of his public image was not consistent with reality. He was living a lie that he himself told to appeal to voters. Journalists had gotten behind the mask of the married, family man and exposed a pattern of behavior extending beyond a weekend dalliance with another woman. Other relationships became known. People quit counting. Questions about character and credibility would forever haunt any steps he might try to take in public life.

Then, a few months after the revelations about Hart, Senator Joseph Biden of Delaware, another Democratic aspirant to the presidential nomination, faced his own questions about the veracity of certain elements of the image he projected. The impressive academic achievements of his college and law school days which he had talked about were discovered to be romanticized recollections of a very average educational career. His prowess as an orator had already come in for scrutiny when it was reported that some of his speeches benefited from unacknowledged passages that had previously appeared in addresses delivered by Robert Kennedy, Hubert Humphrey, and Neil Kinnock, the Labor Party leader in Great Britain. Like Hart, what Biden presented as attractive "image" characteristics or traits were not in keeping with reality. Unlike Hart, Biden quickly withdrew from the campaign and did not return after having second thoughts.

Republican candidates were not immune to image-probing. In the late fall of 1987, it was disclosed that Pat Robertson's first child was born a matter of weeks before his marriage. Reporting this piece of news, which many people believed to be an invasion of privacy, raised questions about the accuracy of the image the minister-politician was projecting. In his religious sermons and political speeches, Robertson had branded pre-marital sex as the devil's play, profane indulgence in a sacred act. Now the nation learned that the reverend's words postdated his own deeds. Robertson tried to dismiss the issue by lashing out at the media and by saying his past included a period of sowing "wild oats." Despite the revelation, Robertson retained his core of faithful followers and remained in the campaign. Public doubts, however, lingered, and his base of support never widened.

Late in his life, Mark Twain wrote, "Everyone is a moon, and has a dark side which he never shows to anybody." The statement is characteristically cynical, yet it rightly recognizes that every person has a private life that deserves to be kept private. Freedom *from* the press is as much a right as freedom *of* the press. Although they relinquish much of their privacy by engaging in public life, political figures are no less deserving than anyone else. Increasingly today, however, questions arise over where to draw the line between the public and the private dimensions of one figure's singular life. Who most appropriately determines what is truly relevant? What process should be followed? Is every piece of soiled underwear from one's past and present worth washing and hanging out to dry in full view of the country? Should an ethical (rather than legal) statute of limitations operate, preventing disclosure of impertinent material with no bearing on someone's public performance?

Establishing a precise line for fair, responsible interplay between journalists and political figures is by no means an exact science. Each case presents its own unique circumstances. It is certainly important for reporters seriously to scrutinize the life history of a public figure to see if there are inconsistencies or discrepancies between that figure's projected image, his or her conscious self-definition, and the reality of the life as it has been lived. Should there be fictive self-inventions, then people have a right to know such information. If, on the other hand, a private matter has occurred in someone's past and it has absolutely no relevance to that person's public life (or even image) today, why should it receive attention? How many worthy people will abandon any desire of potential public service, either elective or appointed, out of fear that a long-ago incident, which could be interpreted negatively, will be revealed?

In Robert Penn Warren's novel *All the King's Men*, Willie Stark, governor, boss, and hardball politician, tells his assistant Jack Burden to dig up some damaging material about an opponent. "There is always something," Willie asserts. When Jack says that might not be the case with this person, a respected judge from Jack's hometown, Willie responds with a hot-tempered yet coldly realistic remark: "Man is conceived in sin and born in corruption and he passeth from the stink of the didie to the stench of the shroud. There is always something."

In his own colorful way, Willie reminds Jack that human perfection is impossible. The realization, too, is a fact of political life. In *Federalist Paper* 51, Madison wrote, "If men were angels, no government would be necessary." Exactly two hundred years later, in the wake of the scandal that led to Hart's demise, Senator Paul Simon of Illinois, himself a candidate for the nomination, said: "We're running for the presidency, not for sainthood."

Recognizing the existence of our fallibility is elementary school material. For people in journalism, making decisions whether or not to divulge someone's "something," to use Willie's word, requires more advanced thinking. Making distinctions is critical. Unless there is a compelling *public reason* to reveal a piece of information about a political figure or governmental official, such coverage does little more than pander or titillate. Voyeurism and journalism are — or should be — different pursuits. However, if lies or half-truths decorate someone's biography to enhance an image or a person engages in private conduct that raises legitimate questions about character and judgment, then the public is ill-served if journalists do not report this kind of material. Hypocrisy is a cardinal sin in political life.

The Age of Personality is not only a period of image dominance; it is also a time of intense interest in "personal ethics." In recent years, the nominations of a Supreme Court Justice (Douglas Ginsburg) and a Secretary of Defense (John Tower) failed to gain Senate approval because of personal rather than policy considerations. In the case of Ginsburg, the smoking of marijuana in his past prevented the possibility of confirmation. With Tower, a fondness for alcohol and women destroyed his chances of serving in the cabinet in such a sensitive post. In the House of Representatives, only days apart in the spring of 1989, the Speaker Jim Wright and the Democratic Whip Tony Coelho resigned their offices after questions and charges about their handling of their own financial affairs.

Whether any of these figures was the victim of unfair treatment by investigatory governmental institutions or inquisitive news media is not the issue here. What is relevant is the fact that an absorption in "personal ethics" is, in part, another consequence of this Age of Personality. A fixation on the individual leads to a concentration of scrutiny on prior behavior, present activities, and future prospects for performance. This process of examination takes places within the wider culture, where personalities in entertainment or sports or business are exposed for living lives that are anything but morally exemplary. The footprints from clay feet are easy to track in Washington and everywhere else political life is conducted. The close scrutiny of someone on the public stage now exists as part of the accepted rite of passage and of continuing performance.

This, however, is *not* to say people in popular communications make it part of their business to "go after" or "get" certain individuals because of either personal animosity or ideological impurity. (Conspiracy theorists are free to indulge their fantasies, but the exercise comes at the expense of genuine knowledge.) A story — such as Gary Hart's or John Tower's — begins as a journalistic or governmental revelation, and then takes on a life of its own. Wall-to-wall coverage results as different media sources scramble to keep up with the newest information. The perception of "press hounding" results from the number of media outlets pursuing the story and from the intensity of coverage they provide. These are institutional factors, aspects of a communications environment that emphasizes personality characteristics. Once there are variations between what we now know of a person and what we previously perceived, the media and the public seek a more realistic view. While the lifestyle of an entertainment or athletic star merely prompts an indulgent fascination or an attitude of "who cares?", the lessons of the 1980s for public figures are quite different. In the political realm, individual moral conduct does matter. Probing relevant "personal ethics" becomes one way of maintaining accountability for those exercising power and authority. It is also a collective realization that an image is *not* necessarily the person and that no one in public life should be taken at face value.

In *Choosing Our King*, Michael Novak writes,

> There is a critical difference between public relations image-making and genuine symbolic engagement. The one is manipulation from outside-in; the other is expression from inside-out. The one tries to execute a prior construct or design; the other tries to allow what is inside to manifest itself. The one tries to guide the reactions of observers; the other tries to make contact with them, so as to liberate energies within them.[4]

Novak's shrewd insight, written before the conclusion of the Watergate saga, appears in his discussion of Richard Nixon's "confusion of public relations imagery with genuine symbols." A similar charge could be made about Jimmy Carter.

Interestingly, for all of the commentary on the image-orientation of Ronald Reagan, much of the popular appeal and success of his two terms as president derived from his "genuine symbolic engagement" and his ability to maintain that engagement. People might have disagreed over individual policies or been confounded by the hypocritical duplicity of the Iran *contra* affair, but the values he stood for and defended in speeches and actions were deeply rooted in core national beliefs — the soul of America. To be sure, public occasions were highly scripted and heavily produced — stagecraft as well as image-making were primary considerations — but the symbolic chords he struck had considerable substantive consequences on the statecraft of his eight-year presidency. Possibly without knowing it, Reagan proved that political leadership demands something more than projecting a winning image.

3

The Bully Pulpit at Center Stage

As Ronald Reagan prepared to leave office, every journalistic medium weighed in with a farewell. Among these valedictory assessments, one reporter quoted Gerald Ford as saying "He is one of the few political leaders I have ever met whose public speeches revealed more than his private conversations." Unremarkable at first reading, the former president's observation of Reagan suggests the opportunities and limitations of stagecraft as a defining component of conducting statecraft.

Throughout the years of the Reagan presidency, surveys of public opinion repeatedly showed wide disparity between approval for Reagan policies and the popularity of the president himself. Support of specific proposals and actions (concerning, for example, the growth of the military, the cutting back of domestic programs, or expanding deregulation) lagged well behind the personal affection for the man responsible for the policies. This paradoxical, public-of-two-minds phenomenon also extended to the people Reagan wanted in office to support his measures. In the fall of 1986 — shortly after *Time* did a cover story about the president that attempted to answer "Why Is This Man So Popular?"— Reagan personally campaigned for ten Republican candidates for the Senate and House of Representatives. Nine lost their races, and the Democrats took control of the Senate for the first time since the election of 1980.

Reagan's ability to be perceived as distinct from his policies and from the people associated with him reflects the dominance of personality in contemporary American political life. It is as if the audience does not care for the play or for the supporting cast, but remains mesmerized by the leading performer. Reagan brought to state and national politics considerably more than his experience as a radio announcer, an actor in the movies, or genial host of television shows or nightclub routines. He elevated the use of the popular forms of communication to a level never before attempted or attained. Sophisticated stagecraft helped keep control of the national agenda and attention while also advancing what the administration sought to achieve as statecraft.

In *The Rhetorical Presidency*,[1] Jeffrey Tulis, a political scientist, traces the evolution and implications of "popular or mass rhetoric" as "a principal tool of presidential governance." He shows that direct appeals to the people did not begin until the early years of this century, at about the time Theodore Roosevelt recognized that the "presidency is a bully pulpit." Since Roosevelt and Woodrow Wilson sought to go over the heads of Congress and to establish themselves as political personalities in continuing communication with the citizenry, presidential leadership has changed dramatically. Occupants of the White House have become much more concerned about maintaining a connection with the people at large rather than delivering formal, governmental messages, such as those presented periodically to Congress. By using the various forms of popular, mass communications, presidents throughout this century have reasoned they could actively shape and mold the public opinion necessary to strengthen their power either for policy action or for re-election. Presidential emphasis on people-oriented, mediated leadership has had an effect on all government, influencing how legislators, governors, mayors, and even appointed public officials conduct themselves and transact the people's business. The integration of sophisticated polling surveys into the day-to-day activities and decisions of political figures makes constant feedback possible. Messages can be tailored for the immediate, favorable reaction.

In the presidential realm, the Reagan years provide a rich case study in the evolving techniques of leadership through mass media. What earlier presidents began and tried to foster, Reagan raised to a form of popular art. The presidency itself was not only rhetorical but theatrical, with daily performances part of the strategy. Although White House reporters groused about the infrequency of press conferences—fewer than fifty over eight years—such criticism had little impact. Reagan and the people around him had their own ideas about portraying the presidency. They would do whatever they could to project what they wanted the public to see and to hear. Planned (scripted) occasions were always less risky than a tightrope-walk in front of the press corps.

Several commentators on Reagan as president have drawn parallels to Franklin Roosevelt's mastery of the media, especially his use of the radio with his "Fireside Chats." Similarities exist—both leaders maintained rapport with the citizenry through strategic communication directed to people's homes—but Reagan's efforts had a much different pace and pattern. During his twelve years as president, Roosevelt delivered twenty-seven "Fireside Chats," while holding 998 press conferences (an average of 6.9 per month). By contrast, Reagan conducted a weekly radio broadcast for eight years, and it was a rare day when (either at work or on vacation) he did not receive television coverage on all of the networks. There was, according to his public relations-minded staff, a "line of the day" that contributed to the process of presidential leadership. That line, carefully selected and serving a specific purpose, would come, substantively, in remarks the president might make or, symbolically, in what he might do. Even those hazy telephoto shots of Reagan on horseback or clearing brush on his California ranch delivered a definite message—this oldest of presidents was naturally vigorous away from the White House as well as in it.

Ronald Reagan was an abiding presence, albeit on his terms. If he (or those around him) wanted to get a point across, the president had a glib, quotable one-liner at the ready for the television cameras to record. If pictures were enough to convey the desired impression, then the president could jauntily stride to the helicopter or back to the White House, while journalists, kept at an administration-approved safe distance away, unsuccessfully shouted questions at the smiling, thumbs-up figure. Reagan always knew when he was "on" and where the cameras were. Throughout his eight years in office, it is difficult to find television coverage or printed pictures that are not appropriate for the occasion or generally reassuring. The shots of him leaving the last session of the 1986 summit with Mikhail Gorbachev in Reyk-javik, Iceland, show disgust and failure, but they are atypical.

The visual imperative of television helped keep the nation's focus on Reagan as both president and personality. Unlike his four immediate predecessors (Lyndon Johnson, Richard Nixon, Gerald Ford, and Jimmy Carter) he did not seem to wear out his welcome in our living rooms. The dominant medium of com-munications had a national leader to cover who enjoyed mixing business and pleasure, governing and entertaining. Martin Schram tells a story about fellow journalist Lesley Stahl that em-phasizes the Reagan people's understanding of television and how to use it. On October 4, 1984, a month before Reagan faced Wal-ter Mondale at the polls, Stahl put together a detailed report for the *CBS Evening News*. Throughout the nearly six-minute story — more than triple the length of a standard package — Stahl talked about the discrepancies between the symbolism of the Reagan presidency and the reality of the Reagan policies. The strongly worded script made the reporter apprehensive about ad-ministration reaction. However, instead of being critical, the Reagan people were delighted. An unnamed assistant told Stahl: "We're in the middle of a campaign and you gave us four and a half minutes of great pictures of Ronald Reagan. And that's all the American people see. . . . They don't listen to you if you're contradicting great pictures. They don't hear what you are say-ing if the pictures are saying something different."[2]

Stahl's story has been repeated so many times by chroniclers of the Reagan years and by analysts of the politics-media rela-tionship that it has assumed the status of contemporary legend. It well illustrates a principal problem television faces as an in-strument of communication. We tend to believe what we *see* — which is the main reason television news has higher credibility than other sources — and engaging visuals carry their own mean-ings, frequently quite distinct from the words we might hear. The eye overrides the ear. If there is conflict between what we are shown and what we are told, a high percentage of the viewing audience will not analyze the dissonant elements and resolve the seemingly different messages.

The CBS report was a sincere attempt to do something net-work broadcasts are accused of rarely trying — a probing examina-tion of a subject not confined to the usual 90-second treatment.

David Broder reports that "Stahl said she looked at the piece again, with the sound off, and realized that what she had shown was a magnificent montage of Reagan in a series of wonderful, upbeat scenes, with flags, balloons, children, and adoring supporters—virtually an unpaid campaign commercial." When Broder asked Stahl whether the experience had changed the way she did her stories, she replied: "Not really. I'm still trapped, because my pieces are written to the pictures we have."[3] And those pictures, to a great degree, were produced *by* the White House *for* the president. A new phrase, "the art of the backdrop," crept into discussions of the staging of events involving Reagan. Every setting for an appearance was strategically made to reinforce the intended impression or to create a sense of drama. Little was left to chance or improvisation.

Even a speech to dedicate a new stamp became a presidential playlet, complete with an array of telegenic moments for network use. In March 1988, Reagan visited the University of Notre Dame, when a stamp honoring the University's former football coach Knute Rockne was first issued. As formal proceedings began, the president had not appeared on the stage, provoking puzzlement among the assembled. Some scenes from the 1940 movie *Knute Rockne—All American* were shown on a large screen behind the dais, with several scenes featuring the young actor Ronald Reagan as George Gipp. The film includes not only the death of the talented running back Gipp—hence the death-bed line "Win one for the Gipper"—but the fatal airplane crash involving Rockne that occurred in 1931. The funeral scene, with a priest eulogizing the coach, has a line that says, "Ask the president of the United States."

With those words spoken, the film abruptly stopped and the band struck up "Hail to the Chief," bringing Reagan triumphantly to the platform. After delivering a characteristically positive speech on the worth of education and the need for a commitment to moral values, he seemed to take genuine delight in moving away from the lectern to toss a football into the crowd. And cameras recorded the gesture for action-absorbed audiences. The appearance, just a routine occasion on the president's schedule, was clearly planned with two audiences in mind—the few thousand attending the event and the millions who would learn about it through the media, especially television. On both levels the production focused on Reagan as both president and personality — the uplifting leader with natural entertainment skills.

During the Reagan years, Theodore Roosevelt's concept of the presidency as "bully pulpit" took on greater meaning than ever before. The Reagan staff took to heart Shakespeare's line, "All the world's a stage," and continually designed occasions to conform to their purposes. George Reedy, former press secretary to Lyndon Johnson and now a journalism professor, notes that "the transition from pulpit to stage is one of the more significant trends in modern history." He goes on to say: "A pulpit is a platform for persuasion and exhortation. A stage is a setting for a presentation that may or may not carry a message. It can be an instrument for education and leadership or an attention-getting device for entertainment."[4]

From 1981 until 1989, Reagan and the people around him used both the pulpit *and* the stage, attempting to cover all the different possibilities (persuasion, exhortation, education, leadership, entertainment) simultaneously. Sometimes the strategy would misfire — notably the controversial May 1985 visit to Bitburg, Germany, to a cemetery which included the graves of S.S. officers. That event was first conceived for its potentially positive public relations value — to honor the war dead of a former enemy who has now become a trusted ally. Characteristically Reagan did not let the impassioned criticism from such figures as Nobel Peace Prize winner Elie Wiesel change his mind — he went to the cemetery — and years later he still defended the decision. In *Speaking My Mind*, Reagan said in a headnote to the text of his Bitburg remarks: "When our advance people had gone over, snow covered the SS graves so our people didn't see them. . . . Later, I also learned that several of the Nazi storm troopers buried there were buried in prisoner uniforms. They were killed by their fellow SS members for helping concentration camp prisoners. I received letters to this effect from Jewish survivors."[5] The explanation is typical of the man's abiding attitude — "It was not my fault and, besides, the critics were wrong in the first place."

Popular approval of Reagan fluctuated during his two terms, with sharp drops coming during the 1981–82 recession and the Iran-*contra* fiasco that began to unfold in late 1986. But in these cases and others, Reagan bounced back into public favor after spending some time in the national doghouse. Unlike Johnson,

Nixon, and Carter, Reagan was able to avoid irreversible public disfavor. To a considerable degree, policy initiatives (for example, measures to stimulate the economy and governmental investigations to discover what John Poindexter and Oliver North were doing *in* Iran and *to* Nicaragua) helped Reagan to rebound. However, in addition there was the president's own personality, complete with a certain telegenic charisma, that continued to command the broadcast airwaves. He kept talking about "standing tall" and a rekindling of American patriotism.

As Garry Wills observes, rather than George Gipp, the player, Reagan was more like Knute Rockne, the coach, encouraging a nation to remember its past in building the present and future.[6] These pep talks conformed to the dominant medium (television) and to the messenger (Reagan). They were easy to understand, even conversational, and dramatic enough to appeal to the public's emotions. Some occasions — such as the speech after the explosion of the space shuttle *Challenger* in 1986 and the address in France to honor the fortieth anniversary of D-Day in 1984 — stand out as especially memorable moments. These events might dwarf others, but they were part of a continuing stream of words and gestures produced for both substantive and symbolic effect.

When Reagan left the presidency, his approval rating (according to the *Gallup Report*) was 63 percent. The figure was up from its low point of 35 percent (in January 1983 amid the economic recession) and down somewhat from a high of 68 percent (reached in May of both 1981 and 1986). Reagan's popularity as he concluded his presidency stood in contrast to the surveys of job approval for his predecessors. Although the last survey of public opinion about FDR showed 66 percent approval, none of the other presidents' last approval ratings went above 60 percent — Carter at 34 percent, Ford at 53 percent, Nixon at 24 percent, Johnson at 49 percent, Kennedy at 58 percent, Eisenhower at 59 percent, and Truman at 31 percent.

It is possible, however, to make too much of polls of public approval and effectively orchestrated events that played well on television. Historians may find it difficult to deal with the Reagan presidency because its orientation was so overwhelmingly to the "line of the day" and to how that line would be treated by the media, especially network television with its visual imperative. As much as possible, the administration maintained control of the message agenda, and the glass was always half-full, never half-empty. Clearly, there were substantive accomplishments (better economic conditions for many, stronger defense capabilities, easing of tensions with the Soviet Union), but at the same time serious problems began to fester (the national debt ballooned, drug usage and drug-related violence grew, the trade imbalance mounted). In addition, the Iran-*contra* scandal, the assorted ethical lapses at the Department of Housing and Urban Development, and the problems in the savings and loan industry raised questions of effective governmental leadership and management. Who was in charge, and what does it mean to be in charge in the context of the modern presidency? As more is learned about the Reagan years, his standing could well be drawn into serious question. Just seven months after leaving the White House, the Gallup Organization conducted a "believability" study for the Times Mirror Center for the People and the Press. Some 53 percent of the 1,507 people surveyed said Reagan was *not* believable, while 47 percent did find him believable — a sizable decline from earlier studies.

Much of the appeal of Ronald Reagan as president can be explained by the positive feelings he generated and kept reinforcing in public — and in front of the media. There was a substantive theme (government is the problem rather than the solution), but the presidency was largely inspirational and atmospheric. Helping to shape a national mood or spirit in stark contrast to the dark times of the Vietnam War, the Watergate affair, and the Iranian hostage crisis is no small achievement. There are, however, profound long-term limitations to a leadership-through-public-appearance approach. Effective governance involves not only successful stagecraft but also adroit statecraft away from the lights and cameras. Here the already-quoted remark of Gerald Ford takes on pertinence. That Ford's "private conversations" with Reagan revealed less than the "public speeches" indicates the disparity between informal exchanges — about policy and political matters of common interest — and the formal, staff-arranged appearances.

In *Presidential Power: The Politics of Leadership from FDR to Carter*, Richard Neustadt quotes the famous lament of Harry Truman: "'I sit here all day trying to persuade people to do the things they ought to have sense enough to do without my persuading them. . . . That's all the powers of the President amount to'." Neustadt, a political scientist, explains:

> The President of the United States has an extraordinary range of formal powers, of authority in statute law and in the Constitution. Here is testimony that despite his "powers" he does not obtain results by giving orders — or not, at any rate, merely by giving orders. He also has extraordinary status, *ex officio*, according to the customs of our government and politics. Here is testimony that despite his status he does not get action without argument. Presidential *power* is the power to persuade.[7]

Reagan's power to persuade was primarily directed outward — through the media to the people. The bond was strong enough, especially until late 1986, that members of Congress and others were reluctant to be critical of the president. Now, however, from the accounts of administration officials and memoirs of congressional leaders, we know that Reagan was less commanding in meetings where policies were being discussed. In fact, his lack of involvement in the internal workings of his administration is a large blot on his record. He could lead a nation to think better about itself, but he could not persuade many of those closest to him to avoid either acts or the appearance of impropriety.

New York Governor Mario Cuomo has said, "We campaign in poetry and govern in prose." For eight years Reagan tried to govern with a poetry of words and body language that popular forms of communication transmitted across the country and around the world. As uplifting as poetry might be, there are times and occasions for clear, detailed prose that explains a complex situation. Rhetoric and symbolism are not enough, especially when others working in the government have their own personal agendas and priorities.

Only the most sheltered and devout Democrat would dispute the fact that some of the positive feelings Reagan enjoyed arose from the emotions he evoked in public appearances during his eight years in the White House. What he did gave new meaning to the phrase "duties *performed* in office." But in looking back at this president and this time, it is curious the extent to which those around Reagan sought to claim credit for those public appearances and their consequences. In the memoirs by Michael Deaver, Larry Speakes, and Donald Regan there is the obligatory bowing and scraping in the direction of the former employer (who was still president when the books were published). These writers, however, are not shy about explaining *their* role in helping Reagan use both the bully pulpit and the world stage. They do not shout out that the emperor paraded around without clothes on, but they do let us know their responsibility for scripting and stage managing specific moments. It is as though some of the people behind the curtain want to get some applause for themselves.

A conspicuous example of this phenomenon is the self-promotion of speechwriter Peggy Noonan. To say that she took authorial pride in the work she did for Reagan would be an understatement. Reporters were dutifully informed that *she* wrote certain speeches (such as the ones after the *Challenger* disaster and the D-Day remembrance), and that fact appeared in the coverage and commentary of the events themselves. An *Esquire* profile of her which appeared in December 1985 carried the title "Who Puts the Words in the President's Mouth?" and led the "Politics and Law" section of an issue about "America's New Leadership Class." To make sure no one forgot her accomplishments as a most visible ghostwriter, Noonan even wrote a book, *What I Saw at the Revolution: A Political Life in the Reagan Era.* One sentence from it offers her, after-the-stage-lights-dim attitude towards Reagan:

> There were times when I would see the earnest young people in the middle levels of the administration trying to get someone to listen to their thoughts, fighting to advance ideas that were not country club but human, and compassionate, and see the sunny president who did not seem to know or notice, and I would think to myself (if I was tired enough, frustrated enough) that the battle for the mind of Ronald Reagan was like the trench warfare of World War I: Never have so many fought so hard for such barren terrain.[8]

The refrain of the backstage chorus indicates both puppetry and ventriloquism. For some political figures such suggestions would be damaging, possibly fatal. But that was not the case with Reagan. The public had a definite perspective of him after years of exposure of various kinds, and his personality dominated public occasions. Others might have written the words or designed the stage, but he made the appearances *his*. That staff people wanted some glory had little (if any) impact on what the mass public thought and felt.

Reagan's success at popular leadership primarily through popular communications stands in stark contrast to the efforts of his predecessor Carter. With that reassuring smile and what Marshall McLuhan called the "spontaneous casualness" necessary for television, Carter emerged in late 1975 and early 1976 as a politician different from those populating the post-Watergate landscape. But as time passed — the rest of 1976 and during his four years in the White House — Americans found it increasingly difficult to understand him and his thinking.

Carter and the people around him knew that stagecraft is important to statecraft. Pollster Patrick H. Caddell advised the president early in his term, "Governing with public approval requires a continuing political campaign." In the first few months of the Carter administration, the country saw its new president walk down Pennsylvania Avenue, conduct a town meeting in New England, deliver his version of a Fireside Chat, answer questions phoned in from average folks, allow production of "a day in the life" documentary, as well as meet the press frequently in formal and informal exchanges.

All of this activity led Richard Reeves, the political columnist and author, to write an article for the *New York Times Magazine* (May 15, 1977) with the title "Maestro of the Media: The Prime-Time President." Reeves explains the centrality of television to White House operations, but near the end of the article he introduces an ominous element: "Carter, the star, will probably not survive for more than a season — unless he begins thinking more about getting off television than getting on. Whatever his technical mastery of the monster, it is not his medium — because Jimmy Carter is not a nice man. Nice people, in general, do not get to be Presidents of the United States."

As it turned out, the niceness factor was of less consequence than the growing perception that the Carter emphasis on occasions designed for television were gimmicky efforts at public relations and little else. In several sequences of the cartoon "Doonesbury" and in an article "The Man Behind the Cardigan" for the *New Republic*, Garry Trudeau cleverly lampooned the administration's transparent attempts at cultivating public opinion by creating a "Secretary of Symbolism," who seemed to have more serious responsibilities than other cabinet officers. Ironically, there was more manipulation of the media during the Reagan years, but the results — what the public actually saw and heard — seemed less contrived. There was greater coherence between stagecraft and statecraft, between delivering a definite statement effectively and having that statement advance the policy or political agenda of the Reagan administration.

Public doubt about Jimmy Carter grew as he kept telling the people how problems such as inflation, steep interest rates, and the energy crisis were difficult to solve. There was a distinct, unreassuring whine in the voice, and the smile of the campaign and early stages of the term was not as noticeable. In press conferences and other occasions where he spoke, Carter displayed a mastery of the facts pertaining to any subject raised — no one could have ever accused him of avoiding his homework — but what he thought and how that thinking translated into policy lacked the clear articulation required of effective leadership through persuasion. In "The Passionless Presidency," Carter's former chief speechwriter James Fallows said that there were times when divergent views were left unreconciled, leading to governmental and public confusion. Fallows reports that Secretary of State Cyrus Vance and National Security Advisor Zbigniew Brzezinski had two, very different viewpoints about one particular foreign policy matter, U.S. relations with the Soviet Union. Carter asked for memos from each person, and then stapled the two statements together, presenting them in a single speech at the U.S. Naval Academy.[9]

By mid-1979 (and facing a campaign to seek re-election in 1980), Carter and the people around him realized that it was necessary to do something bold to assert presidential leadership — and to respond to the public's uneasiness about the president's efforts. Caddell, the pollster and a key adviser, told those in the administration that his survey research revealed national self-doubt, a crisis of faith and confidence. A primary reason for this attitude was the energy crisis, with the resultant increase in prices and long lines at gas stations. (Freedom-loving and car-crazy

Americans felt constrained by oddly dressed figures in countries far away.) A measure of our independence was threatened as the nation became more dependent on foreign producers of oil. Over the objections of Vice President Walter Mondale, chief domestic adviser Stuart Eizenstat, and others, Carter cancelled a speech about the energy problems to focus on the larger socio-political concern Caddell had identified. For ten days, Carter met at Camp David with government officials, business and labor leaders, religious figures, journalists, and educators. On July 15, the president faced the nation and delivered what has become known as "the malaise speech," although the word malaise was never uttered.

Carter's grim manner reflected the substance of what he told an audience estimated at 60 million people. Early in the address he said:

> So, I want to speak to you first tonight about a subject even more serious than energy or inflation. I want to talk to you right now about a fundamental threat to American democracy.
>
> I do not mean our political and civil liberties. They will endure. And I do not refer to the outward strength of America, a nation that is at peace tonight everywhere in the world, with unmatched economic power and military might.
>
> The threat is nearly invisible in ordinary ways. It is a crisis of confidence. It is a crisis that strikes at the very heart and soul and spirit of our national will. We can see this crisis in the growing doubt about the meaning of our own lives and in the loss of a unity of purpose for our Nation.
>
> The erosion of our confidence in the future is threatening to destroy the social and the political fabric of America.
>
> The confidence that we have always had as a people is not simply some romantic dream or a proverb in a dusty book that we read just on the Fourth of July. It is the idea which founded our Nation and has guided our development as a people. Confidence in the future has supported everything else — public institutions and private enterprise, our own families, and the very Constitution of the United States. Confidence has defined our course and has served as a link between generations. We've always believed in something called progress. We've always had a faith that the days of our children would be better than our own.
>
> Our people are losing that faith, not only in government

itself but in the ability as citizens to serve as the ultimate rulers and shapers of our democracy. As a people we know our past and we are proud of it. Our progress has been part of the living history of America, even the world. We always believed that we were part of a great movement of humanity itself called democracy, involved in the search for freedom, and that belief has always strengthened us in our purpose. But just as we are losing our confidence in the future, we are also beginning to close the door on our past.

In a nation that was proud of hard work, strong families, close-knit communities, and our faith in God, too many of us now tend to worship self-indulgence and consumption. Human identity is no longer defined by what one does, but by what one owns. But we've discovered that owning things and consuming things does not satisfy our longing for meaning. We've learned that piling up material goods cannot fill the emptiness of lives which have no confidence or purpose.[10]

No one could deny Carter's courage or sincerity in saying what he did. However, the message was both jarring and puzzling. Three years earlier, he had travelled throughout the country, saying at virtually every campaign stop that the United States needed "a government that is as good and honest and decent and competent and compassionate and as filled with love as are the American people." That theme, which struck a chord in the post-Watergate environment, seemed to be replaced with an attitude of *"it's your fault"* that we have a spiritual crisis and national cynicism. Shortly after the speech, with its talk of unity, Carter asked for the resignations of his entire Cabinet, and he disposed of Secretaries Michael Blumenthal (Treasury), Joseph Califano (Health, Education and Welfare), and James Schlesinger (Energy), as well as Attorney General Griffin Bell. The shuffle of the cabinet looked like another attempt to shift blame. The word "malaise" haunted the Carter administration the rest of its term. The Iranian hostage situation, which began in November 1979 and included a failed rescue effort that Carter gently called an "incomplete success," concentrated the public mind on what seemed national helplessness when confronted by a foreign threat. Despite numerous efforts of various kinds, Jimmy Carter could not persuade the people — or many in Congress — that he could lead and govern. There was a hollow sound coming from the bully pulpit. The election of Reagan in 1980 was as much a rejection of Carter as it was a true vote of confidence in the former California governor.

Lessons of the Reagan method — combining statecraft and stagecraft to secure and sustain popular leadership — have been instructive to his successor George Bush. Bush, however, has adapted what he learned as vice president for his purposes and his own personality. Throughout the campaign of 1988, he followed the Reagan method faithfully — journalists' access was tightly controlled, speeches were peppered with unnuanced, tough-sounding one-liners for television reports, and large American flags were strategically placed around many of the speaking sites to symbolize (again for television) an unwavering patriotism.

Remarkably, though, once he won the election by using Reaganesque techniques, Bush began to assert his independence — and his own identity — by conducting himself as president in a much different way. Unlike his predecessor, he placed greater emphasis on a one-on-one style of leadership instead of a mass-mediated approach. Bush worked the telephone and arranged small gatherings at the White House to show his personal involvement and openness. Reporters had more opportunities to engage in question-and-answer periods, with these occasions designed to be informational rather than the irregular, carefully produced affairs of the Reagan years. There was less concern for creating a "line of the day" and prime-time occasions. According to a study by the Center for Media and Public Affairs, Bush in his first year received *one-third* the network television coverage that Reagan received during his first year.

In the early days of the Bush administration, observers of American political life — if not the public at large — kept wondering "Where is George?" The question was adapted from a speech given by Senator Edward Kennedy at the 1988 Democratic Convention. The crowd-pleasing refrain of "Where was George?" ridiculed Bush's involvement in policy decisions and actions as vice president. That the line was appropriated by Kennedy's speechwriter from H. A. Rey's children's books about "Curious George," the "curious little monkey," went unremarked, but knowing the source gives an even sharper edge to the ridicule.

Some might view presidential invisibility as a blessing; however, it is risky governance at a time when the media occupy the role they do in our political environment. Indeed, shortly after the spate of "Where is George?" inquiries, there was more effort to arrange events that would generate news coverage. Bush's speech advocating a constitutional amendment outlawing desecration of the flag, which he gave June 30, 1989, took place at the Iwo Jima Memorial in Arlington, Virginia, and looked remarkably similar to several of his 1988 campaign appearances. Two trips to Europe (in spring and summer of 1989) also commanded public attention more effectively than an earlier excursion to the Far East or some of his domestic travels across the country. One earlier trip to the Midwest and Far West had been so frenetic and ill-planned that it proved almost impossible to cover.

Seven months into his presidency, in September 1989, George Bush delivered his first prime-time speech to the nation from the Oval Office, announcing his administration's plans to combat drugs. Response to the address was, at best, lukewarm. When it was revealed that a bag of cocaine he held up as a prop for the visually dependent medium of television — "This is crack cocaine seized a few days ago by Drug Enforcement Administration agents in a park just across the street from the White House" — had been picked up at the explicit direction of a member of the president's staff for the sake of the speech, snickers were heard across the land. Revealingly, just a few days before this self-described "heart-to-heart" talk, Bush confessed to David Frost in an interview for the Public Broadcasting System, "I'm not good at expressing the concerns of a nation — I'm just not very good at it."

Bush, however, is not an easy political leader to analyze and to evaluate. During his years as vice president, Washington insiders asserted that he was "a hollow man." The *there* just was not there in Bush and the lack of a defining, animating political core stood in sharp juxtaposition to Reagan, who (for better or worse) had distinct beliefs or values that shaped him and his presidency. But Bush's election campaign and his first year-and-a-half in office render the charge of being "hollow" either wrong or obsolete, a misinterpretation of the man's potential to move from the Gipper's cheerleader to the nation's coach. However, Bush himself repeatedly acknowledges in a self-mocking way his problem with "the vision thing"— a difficulty in presenting a compelling, coherent message that gives Americans a definite view of where he wants to help take the country.

This absence of vision might trouble some political observers, but it clearly does not bother most people. Near the mid-point of his term, popularity and approval surveys approach 80 percent in support of Bush. This high standing, according to some analysts, is the consequence of a relatively good economy at home, of the capitulation of communism abroad, and of the military success in Panama that took place in December 1989. There is much truth in this assessment, but it does not probe deeply enough into a more complete understanding of George Bush and his presidency. He is considerably more complex than the what-you-see-is-what-you-get figure he projects through the media, especially television.

During the Reagan years, the White House seemed like a theater stage or movie set, complete with a star who combined statecraft and stagecraft in a deliberate, politically purposeful way. The previously discussed "line of the day" contributed to an overall script that shaped the substance and symbolism of that presidency. Since Bush was inaugurated in early 1989, the White House has undergone major metaphorical remodelling. Now it is more accurate to think of the White House as a grand orchestra hall, accommodating a full complement of instruments. Bush, of course, is the conductor. Away from public view (the podium, if you will), he decides what music will be played and how it will be presented. What is striking is the variety in the Bush repertoire, and his ability to achieve harmony while directing the different players and their instruments. Here we confront the little-noted complexity of our conductor-in-chief.

While Bush has quite deliberately cultivated an image of being a "kinder, gentler" person, a lover of puppies and small children and a hater of racism and bigotry, his chief political adviser is Lee Atwater, the Republican National Committee chairman. Atwater, known for his vicious attacks, helped make the black rapist Willie Horton a symbolic issue during the 1988 campaign and raised rumors in the spring of 1989 about the sexual orientation of Representative Tom Foley (D-Wash.), just before he became Speaker of the House. Within the White House, former New Hampshire Governor John Sununu also follows a different approach from the president's. A 1990 *Washington Post* profile of Sununu begins: "In contrast to the kinder, gentler image cultivated by his boss in his first year in office, White House Chief of Staff John H. Sununu has emerged as a bare-knuckles, partisan slugger with a volcanic temper and an aversion to conciliation and compromise."

Although the president has made an effort, unprecedented in recent times, to be open and accessible to journalists through frequent news conferences and individual interviews, there has been secrecy and actual instances of deception within the White House. Secret trips to China by high-ranking officials (despite a stated government ban), Bush's denials of a possible summit with Mikhail Gorbachev (although the Malta meeting had already been scheduled), and repeated statements that he was not contemplating additional troop cuts in Europe (which proved false with his 1990 State of the Union announcement of a force reduction from 275,000 to 195,000) ran counter to genuine openness. In the phrase of a headline in the *Indianapolis Star*, the newspaper owned by Vice President Dan Quayle's family, "Mr. President, you're no George Washington."

This particular situation even provoked presidential pique. En route to a drug summit in Colombia in February 1990, Bush responded to stories about such deception and misdirection by telling reporters aboard Air Force One, "We've got a whole new relationship. I think we've had too many press conferences. It's not good." Several questions brought a litany of "no comment" answers from Bush. Yet following the summit, the president conducted *two* news sessions with journalists.

For most of his first year as president, Bush conducted himself with caution — his word of choice was "prudence"— in dealing with such matters as the upheaval in China and throughout Eastern Europe as well as an aborted coup in Panama that occurred in October 1989. Yet he boldly approved the military intervention in Panama, and he undertook a risky trip to Colombia for the conference on drugs.

The collapse of communism and the end of the Cold War that took place in 1989 and 1990 served not only to reduce East-West tensions but resulted in definite policy decisions to save the government money previously awarded to the Defense Department.

Yet the president made a widely covered three-day western tour in early 1990 to watch war games, complete with "Soviet" tanks, and has spoken out on behalf of continuing the funding of the Strategic Defense Initiative.

While Bush states his aspirations of being known as "the education president" and "the environmental president," his administration's 1991 federal budget shortchanged his 1990 State of the Union goals for the year 2000 of a 90 percent graduation rate from high school and American students "first in the world in math and science achievement" by not even keeping pace with inflation. Despite a proposal to elevate the Environmental Protection Agency to a cabinet-rank department, the president and his administration signaled governmental retreat on several fronts in 1990. Instead of initiating sustained action on global warming and increasing protection of wetland areas — expected measures from what the president had said earlier — Bush advocated more research before implementing definite policies.

Other such examples exist. To some observers the specific cases might represent paradoxical contradictions, several visions in conflict. It is more accurate to see what is happening as deliberate orchestration by a talented conductor attempting to hit specific notes that reverberate for distinct constituencies in this diverse country. Piccolos for peace one day, followed by some thumps on a kettledrum to warn of war a few days later. Point, counterpoint.

Given the popular standing of the president at this time (mid-1990), it is clear that few Americans detect any dissonance — no clashing cymbals (or symbols) that are unduly jarring. But it is also clear that reading the president's lips will take citizens just so far. As the months pass, we will all need to watch and listen to the whole performance to see whether George Bush is, indeed, a maestro.

The prime question is: Can a leader effectively govern today without commanding the instruments of popular communication? The answer is yes — but only up to a point. There are times (for example, during a domestic or foreign crisis) when an inspirational style is just as important as the substance of policy. If a leader fails to project intensity and urgency, the message will not be persuasive or rallying — the impact on public opinion and how seriously everyone responds to the appeal will be diminished.

Popular leadership does not mean that there is one, definite way of governing. It does mean that since the focus is on the individual personality of the public figure, that figure needs to command attention in a manner perceived to be natural, genuine, and authoritative. Media clutter, the overload of different messages competing for our time at any given moment, makes it increasingly difficult for someone to be certain that a specific message is getting through to the public. Successful political communication requires mastery of the instruments of popular communication. Without this mastery, a public figure endangers his or her ability to lead through persuasion. Without some stagecraft that captures and holds the citizenry-audience, effective statecraft that receives consent of the governed and can stand the test of long-term public good is not possible.

In *Leaders*, Richard Nixon discusses world figures he has known (Winston Churchill, Charles de Gaulle, Nikita Khrushchev, Zhou Enlai), and he offers his "reflections on leadership."

> Television today has transformed the ways in which national leadership is exercised and has substantially changed the kind of person who can hope to be elected to a position of leadership. Abraham Lincoln, with his homely features and high-pitched voice, would never have made it on television. Nor would his speaking style, with its long, rambling anecdotes, have worked on the tube. The premium today is on snappy one-liners, not lengthy parables.[11]

Nixon goes too far. Certain people, for whatever reason, are not congenitally excluded from participating in televised politics in this transformed period in our political life. Lincoln could have learned how to communicate on television. Mastering this medium is "a learnable skill." Lincoln's sincerity and humor would come across effectively; his physical appearance could be improved. And in some areas, no change would be necessary — his Gettysburg Address lasted but a few minutes, with most of the statements in it being of "sound-bite value."

Skillful governance involves resourceful adapting to specific situations and environments. Having the chance to govern means also being attentive to the requirements of the dominant device of projection. Shortly after bowing out of the 1988 presidential campaign as a Democratic candidate, Bruce Babbitt, the former governor of Arizona, told the *Washington Post:*

> I had a problem with television, as everybody knows by now. I said after my first TV debate that if they could teach Mr. Ed to talk on TV, they could teach me. So I went to "charm school," in front of 20 million Americans, to learn things I should have learned 20 years ago. It was really wonderful. Really character-building.
>
> So what did I learn in charm school? Very simple: There is a picture-frame protocol for television that is very different from normal public speaking. If you watch me talking to a small group, you'll see all the problems that were evident on television. I tend to move around, my gestures are too expansive. I'm out of the picture frame. When you watch me on television, you get a sense of being on a roller coaster. So I tried to learn some basic things: Look at your subject. Be conversational. Tone down your gestures. And ultimately, forget about it all and relax.

The lessons Babbitt learned as a candidate are part of today's basic training of any public official whose work receives media coverage.

The rise of television, with its fixation on personality, means that a new set of informal ground rules apply in political communication. One dimension of leadership today is the ability to command attention through the media in a manner that establishes a definite agenda. That agenda, then, becomes a principal concern within government, while the public at large watches what happens with varying degrees of interest. Another dimension involves the use of those same media to inspire the people, in effect establishing the emotional atmosphere of political life.

As significant as strategic, effective use of popular communications might be, there needs to be judicious balance between mediated moments that are outwardly directed and closed-door meetings that internally resolve policy matters as well as monitor day-to-day governmental activities. Without such balance, the leadership runs the risk of being either overly theatrical or unduly remote. To concentrate on leadership through the media can result in conduct that conforms to the present-mindedness of popular communications — in other words, a series of ephem-

eral messages or appeals lacking long-range consideration. However, to subordinate the media component or to handle it poorly
can ultimately lead to others setting the agenda, to an absence
of inspiration, and to a decline of popular approval that makes
leadership electorally impossible.

4

The Momentary Majority

Three years after *Public Opinion* explained that journalism offers a somewhat frayed lifeline to American democracy, Walter Lippmann continued his exploration of the gulf between "beliefs and realities," the theory and practice, in our political life. He described "the private citizen" as someone burdened by an overly romantic conception of public involvement, and he confessed that even he could not meet the expectations of dreamy democrats.

> My sympathies are with [the average citizen] for I believe that he has been saddled with an impossible task and that he is asked to practice an unattainable ideal. I find it so myself for, although public business is my main interest and I give most of my time to watching it, I cannot find time to do what is expected of me in the theory of democracy; that is, to know what is going on and to have an opinion worth expressing on every question which confronts a self-governing community. And I have not happened to meet anybody, from a President of the United States to a professor of political science, who came anywhere near to embodying the accepted ideal of the sovereign and omnicompetent citizen.[1]

After dispensing with the unrealistic, yet utterly American notion of individual supremacy in the public realm, Lippmann looks beyond the citizen to the citizenry, the collective agent of popular will. Once again he stands the sentiment of Fourth of July rhetoric on its head. "These conclusions are sharply at variance with the accepted theory of popular government. That theory rests upon the belief that there is a public which directs the course of events. I hold that this public is a mere phantom. It is an abstraction. . . . The public is not, as I see it, a fixed body of individuals. It is merely those persons who are interested in an affair and can affect it only by supporting or opposing the actors."[2] Lippmann called his sobering, demythicizing study, published in 1925, *The Phantom Public.*

Today the public of knowledgeable, omnicompetent citizens remains phantom. However, discoveries in the social sciences as well as in the use of sophisticated computer technology now make it possible to measure public reaction, if not public judgment or even public opinion, in ways Lippmann could not have envisioned in the 1920s. The design of survey research instruments along with computerized processing of collected data allow those interested in political life, whether participants or analysts, to keep a constant finger on the pulse of the body politic. The capability of monitoring sentiments, reactions, opinions, attitudes, and values along with their behavioral consequences has dramatically changed how public figures conduct themselves — as they seek office and also as they serve.

Rapid, even instantaneous communication and continuous assessment of survey information contribute to the creation of what might be called a "momentary majority." This momentary majority comes into being quickly and possesses the potential for influencing political or governmental decisions and actions. In the stagecraft of statecraft, the way the citizen-audience reacts to one act frequently shapes the execution of the next act, whatever it might be. The momentary quality of this phenomenon can lead to improvisational politics and policy-making as well as a pronounced volatility in the views held within the already phantom public.

Those who use survey research extensively explain that their work enables them to know what people are thinking or feeling at a given time. Polling information *is* instructive, allowing public figures to appear responsive to the thoughts and concerns of the citizenry. To a certain extent, reliance on such data makes the conduct of political life today different from the past — more democratic and less republican. When our governmental system was being established, the Founders wrestled with two competing fears: the fear of an overly powerful governmental structure that would suppress the people and the fear of having the people themselves overly involved in the actual day-to-day operations of government. The compromise that was worked out entrusted the selection of key public officials to the public through regular elections, with those officials responsible for the workings and maintenance of government.

A refrain throughout *The Federalist Papers* is that the people are sovereign, but those people cannot — and should not — govern directly. Republicanism — governance by the elected who are subject to checks and balances as well as periodic approval by electors — addressed the potential problems endemic to direct democracy, such as the possibility of mob rule and the disregarding of minority rights. Nowadays, with the use of survey research integrated into the process of governance, there is less distance between the elected and the electors. As beneficial as this situation might seem, it raises questions about the direction of contemporary political life in America.

In confessing that he failed to meet the expectations of "the sovereign and omnicompetent citizen," Walter Lippmann was also looking beyond himself. If I do not know enough about a certain subject to formulate a reasoned opinion about it, he implicitly asks, what about other people who spend much less time examining public issues? This question leads to the thorny territory of public knowledge and public ignorance. What does the average citizen know, and how well does he or she know it? Recent studies of political and governmental knowledge do little to suggest that the American public is moving closer to the ideal Lippmann described. One academic survey conducted in 1989 showed but a modest gain in this type of knowledge compared to a similar study made forty years ago. Analyzing the responses to twelve key questions, researchers found some 3 percent more of those interviewed correctly dealt with such basic facts as the length of a presidential term and what the first Ten Amendments to the Constitution are called. Only 25 percent (of the 609 adults contacted) were able to name both of the United States senators from their states.

The marginal improvement in political and governmental knowledge today is significant because it is occurring at a time when there is more emphasis on formal education and greater exposure to popular forms of communication and information, especially television. If just over half of the people know merely basic information about our political system, one wonders the extent to which those in public life should use survey research to influence what they do. What is actually being measured? Is it genuine public opinion, or is it more akin to collective guesswork, spur-of-the-moment reaction to a series of multiple-choice questions?

In *The Paradox of Mass Politics: Knowledge and Opinion in the American Electorate*, W. Russell Neuman probes the complex relationships between the people and their political life in this country.[3] Like Lippmann, he contrasts the theory of civic-minded, democratic citizenship, so fundamental to our political culture, with the practice of the real citizenry. Relying on numerous quantitative studies since 1948, Neuman shows how remote vast numbers of Americans are from political concerns. He sees three distinct publics coexisting within the United States — the "apolitical" public (20 percent), the "mass public" (75 percent), and the "activist" public (5 percent). We talk of "government of the people, by the people, for the people"; however, where, politically speaking, are these people? As Neuman asserts, "Public ignorance and apathy seem to be the enduring legacy of twenty-five hundred years of political evolution. This is the paradox of mass politics." Five overlapping factors frame the paradox: "citizen apathy, low levels of political knowledge, unstructured political thought, pseudo opinions, and issueless politics."[4]

Given these realities, it becomes necessary for those in political life to find ways of triggering attention and action by a considerable percentage of people in the "mass public." Stagecraft makes its entrance here, particularly with the studied usage of popular forms of communication to penetrate the ignorance.

For over twenty years, as political speaker, as governor, and as president, Ronald Reagan was criticized for being overly simplistic and repetitive in addressing political issues. Such criticism, of course, comes in large measure from people within the "activist" public, the elite who know more about the complexity of specific problems. However, much of Reagan's success and popularity resulted from his ability to make a connection with citizens in the "mass public." Once his basic political message received acceptance—what he said in 1964 in support of Barry Goldwater for president changed little—he kept driving it home. During Reagan's years in the White House, his pollster, Richard Wirthlin, assembled focus groups to react to presidential speeches and press conferences. Statements greeted with approval were repeated over and over in subsequent appearances; those that failed to strike a chord were dropped. "I helped to make a great communicator half a degree greater," Wirthlin told the *Washington Post*. In campaigning and in governing, Reagan presented himself and his policy initiatives in ways that conformed to the dominant forms of popular communication, using these means to secure a place in the politically unpreoccupied public mind of millions of Americans. The mass media—with their characteristics and requirements, especially their preoccupation with personality—became the vital link to the "mass" public.

By contrast, after campaigning for president in 1976 with an accessible, thematic message of good government with a moral purpose, Jimmy Carter spent much of his term in the White House either saying problems were complex and could not be resolved easily or explaining the actual complexities facing the nation. Neither approach engaged the "mass" public in a meaningful way. There is merit, of course, in articulating complicated matters, but it is also important to state the case in a manner that holds people's attention and contributes to their understanding.

The "paradox of mass politics" is even more puzzling today with the greater availability of political information: newspapers and magazines abound; television networks and radio stations are devoted exclusively to news; the commercial networks and stations as well as the Public Broadcasting Service provide political coverage of some kind on a daily basis. And yet the decade-old public ignorance persists. Determining how to deliver a political message within this environment becomes almost as important as the message itself.

In the realm of electoral politics, Walter Dean Burnham reminds us that "nineteenth-century elections were major sources of entertainment in an age unblessed by modern mass communications, so that it is more difficult for politicians to gain and keep public attention today than it was then."[5] Going to torchlight parades or attending evenings of political speechifying have been replaced in this century by other leisure-time activities, especially the diversions offered by popular communications. According to recent studies, watching television now ranks third behind working and sleeping in the daily regimen for the average American. Political figures need to go where people gather to present their appeals — which means that the television screen becomes today's principal stage.

However, that stage changes as television changes. The structural or institutional demands of this entertainment-oriented, commercially motivated medium dictate how political communication will be carried to the public at large. A primary difference between messages today and those delivered in the 1950s is the actual time devoted to them. Kathleen Hall Jamieson notes that presidential candidates in 1952 bought thirty-minute blocks of time for speeches. "By 1956 the cost of air time and the dwindling attention of the public prompted politicians to purchase five-minute blocks of speaking time. In the 1970s the five-minute speech gave way to the sixty-second ad."[6] During the 1980s, most political spots ran thirty seconds, with some shorter than that.

In television news on the three major networks, there is a similar pattern of compression. Brevity is a cardinal principle of television. To receive coverage, especially on the most heavily watched evening newscasts, a public figure has to deliver a message in a sentence or two. Detailed discussions of complex issues are boiled down to simplistic slogans or clever quips as public discourse devolves into unilluminating battles of one-liners. A study conducted at the Joan Shorenstein Barone Center on the Press, Politics, and Public Policy of Harvard University found that the average sound-bite on network newcasts during the 1988 campaign was 9.8 seconds. Twenty years earlier, when Richard Nixon ran against Hubert Humphrey, the average was 42.3 seconds of uninterrupted utterance.[7]

T ime is not the only factor. The tone of the political communication is also critically significant, with television's values occupying center stage. American politics has always been not only the competition of ideas about public policy but a blood sport, testing physical and psychological fortitude. Almost two hundred years ago, Federalist newspapers warned citizens what America with Thomas Jefferson as president would be like. "Murder, robbery, rape, adultery and incest will be openly taught and practiced," they partisanly predicted. Just over a hundred years ago, the presidential race in 1884 between Republican Senator James G. Blaine of Maine and Democratic Governor Grover Cleveland of New York featured two spirited and endlessly repeated chants. Democrats shouted, "Blaine! Blaine! James G. Blaine! Continental liar from the state of Maine!" Republicans, who referred to the Democrats as the party of "rum, Romanism, and rebellion," roared back at rallies with a cheer that accused Cleveland of fathering an illegitimate child, "Ma! Ma! Where's my pa? Going to the White House. Ha! Ha! Ha!"

In the past, however, the political dirt flew in more or less contained environments — within party publications or at party-sponsored rallies. A citizen had to show some kind of interest or make some kind of effort to be exposed to these political assaults. Today the mud-slinging is carried into our homes via television. Since political messages, both on news programs and as paid commercials, compete for the public's attention with all of the other messages on television, they are forced to conform to whatever unofficial rules or standards are operating within television at a given time.

The 1964 presidential campaign between Lyndon Johnson and Barry Goldwater was a prime example of the use of "attack" or "negative" advertising on television. People working for Johnson attempted to portray Goldwater as a conservative ideologue, whose election would endanger government programs and risk the possibility of nuclear war. The celebrated "Daisy" commercial, which showed a little girl pulling petals from a flower followed by the jarring scene of an exploding bomb and mushroom cloud, demonstrated the impact this kind of advertising could have. This particular spot aired just once — but that was enough to have its own explosive effect.

The value of negative advertising was proven again in subsequent elections and was relied upon heavily in the 1988 presidential race between George Bush and Michael Dukakis. The Bush victories of the Republican nomination and the White House are textbook examples of positive results by using negative tactics. What Bush and his campaign workers achieved is not only a testament to the effectiveness of such an approach but also a harbinger of what we can expect in American political life in the future. For the many lessons it offers, the 1988 campaign deserves extended analysis.

George Bush went into the New Hampshire primary in February 1988 in a vulnerable position after his third-place showing in the Iowa caucuses a week earlier (behind Senator Robert Dole and Reverend Pat Robertson). In his closing remarks during a New Hampshire debate two days before the primary, Bush said, "I don't talk much, but I do believe. I may not articulate much, but I feel." The vice president did not seem to have much to say on his own. The television ads on his behalf, which were airing repeatedly in New Hampshire, were directed at his rival, Bob Dole. The most-telling spot, a thirty-second ad, accused Dole of straddling issues, such as approving the Intermediate Nuclear Force (INF) treaty, or charging an oil import fee, or raising taxes. At the end of the ad, two faces of Dole dissolve to the words "Taxes — He can't say no," and an announcer chimes in with "Bob Dole straddles, and he just won't promise not to raise taxes. And you know what that means." Dole's lead began to evaporate a few days before the primary.

When Bush won in New Hampshire (with 39 percent to Dole's 29 percent), Dole was asked if he had words for Bush. He tartly responded "Stop lying about my record." Those five words generated several thousand additional ones, as political analysts and operatives for other candidates (especially Bush) said that the remark revealed the mean, embittered Bob Dole. The hatchet man of previous campaigns (namely 1976, when he ran as Gerald Ford's vice presidential candidate) was reemerging after a period when Dole had worked to change how people perceived him and his personality. Doubts about Dole grew quickly after this incident. Lost in the shuffle of this commentary was any consideration that what Dole said might have been true — that his record had, indeed, been distorted by the Bush campaign to gain the advantage in a crucial contest. And, of course, what happened in New Hampshire served as a springboard to the nomination for George Bush.

The most memorable (and repeated) sentence from Bush's acceptance speech at the Republican National Convention in New

Orleans in August 1988 was "I want a kinder, gentler nation." The implicit criticism of the Reagan years contained in that statement went largely unremarked by pundits and Democratic partisans. In addition, it became clear shortly after the convention concluded that the worthy goal of the "kinder, gentler nation" would not be pursued until Dukakis had been defeated.

Bush began his general election effort as an underdog—a summer Gallup Poll showed him behind by 17 percent—and his choice of Indiana Senator J. Danforth Quayle as his vice presidential candidate had produced the opposite of its intended effect. In an attempt to declare his independence from party and press speculation and to select a fresh, telegenic figure, Bush picked Quayle, a youthfully attractive Midwesterner, to spark more interest in the Republican ticket. The spark, however, quickly turned into a firestorm of criticism, as questions about Quayle's education, military service, and suitability to succeed to the presidency multiplied. Meanwhile, his opponent, Michael Dukakis, the governor of Massachusetts, had won the Democratic nomination without becoming that well-known to the public at large, the "mass" public with the greatest number of votes.

The Bush campaign decided it would help America to learn more about Dukakis. Through advertising, primarily on television, and through news coverage of events (visits to flag factories, a boat ride through a polluted Boston harbor, appearances with police groups), Bush developed a negative definition of Dukakis. Even the standard stump speech Bush repeated throughout the country focused on how different he was from his opponent. In mid-September, "The MacNeil/Lehrer NewsHour" on PBS aired the stock Bush speech: a litany of statements attacking Dukakis for furloughing murderers from prison, for opposing the death penalty, for being a "card-carrying member" of the American Civil Liberties Union, for failing to sign a state law mandating the saying of the "Pledge of Allegiance," and for opposing new weapon systems. What George Bush intended to do for his country had to be inferred from his barbed remarks about his opponent.

This negativism prompted doubts and fears. When Dukakis seemed incapable of presenting a compelling message and his campaign performed ineptly, his early, poll-determined support eroded—even more rapidly than it had formed in the late spring and summer. When the votes were counted, the margin of victory for Bush was 8 percent (54 percent to 46 percent), meaning that a full quarter of the electorate changed their minds during the campaign. Such volatility is one primary consequence of our contemporary communications environment and the Age of Personality. To a greater degree than ever before, television played a central role in the 1988 presidential contest. Indeed, the values of television permeated the thinking and actions of everyone involved to the point that commentators talked of the "Made-for-TV Election" and the "Couch Potato Campaign." At times during that autumn, a voter felt trapped in a multi-image, electronic fun-house, where television screens had replaced mirrors. Certain visual scenes kept popping up, but their meaning and context changed with each appearance.

The brief, image-oriented tank excursion that Dukakis took early in the campaign is but one example. What began innocently enough as a staged "media event" to symbolize the candidate's commitment to certain kinds of modern weaponry assumed in videotaped replays a continuing life that Dukakis and his strategists never could have predicted. The first sound of backfire from the ill-fated tank ride was heard on the television networks the evening it took place. Commentators — and comedians — immediately followed with ridiculing assessments, in the main directed at the contrived nature of the occasion and the silly-looking helmet Dukakis wore during the ride. Then, the advertising team working for Bush used the now-familiar tape as the visual backdrop for one of its most telling commercials. The spot's words, both flashed on the screen and spoken, presented doubts about Dukakis's positions on defense matters. That Bush ad — which received considerable attention during news and discussion programs for what many journalists called distortions of the Democrat's views — then became the opening portion of a rebuttal commercial featuring Dukakis himself complaining about negative campaigning. This spot, too, became grist for the video news mill, with the tank-ride tape getting even more mileage.

The visual imperative of television was a primary factor behind the long-running play devoted to the tank outing. The actor and action were incongruous enough to be unintentionally humorous and oddly entertaining. The experience also accommodated television's attraction to conflict, as charges and counter-charges circulated in news broadcasts and through commercials. Conflicts, whether physical or rhetorical, always draw a crowd, and television, whether airing political messages or athletic events, willingly obliges that interest.

The much-discussed negativism surrounding the entire presidential campaign of 1988 can be, in part, traced to this trait of television. Critical and combative statements or ads that play with passions by raising doubts and fears conform to the rapid-fire nature of a "sound-bite" or a thirty-second spot. It takes considerably longer to build an argument about a matter of public policy than to attack an opponent in hit-and-run fashion or to knock down a proposal presented in a caricatured format. Emotions by their nature are volatile, indeed momentary. Television by its nature is a medium that transmits messages of greater emotional than informational impact. In our time the ever-more-complex political and social life with which a citizen has to deal is described by forms of popular communication emphasizing simplification, abbreviation, and other traits to gain attention. Television is not, of course, the only culprit. The success and influence of a newspaper like *USA Today* demonstrate the broad appeal of more reliance on the visual display of information. Walter Lippmann called the first chapter of *Public Opinion* "The World Outside and the Pictures in Our Heads." Increasingly today "the pictures in our heads" come from pictures, moving or still, which leave a valuable imprint. However, their dominance devalues and draws into question the cliché about a picture being worth a thousand words. Eric Sevareid exaggerates when he remarks that "one good word is worth a thousand pictures," but there is more than a kernel of truth in his sentiment.

Who is responsible for this current state of American political life, complete with its negativism and its volatility or momentariness? The question usually provokes finger-pointing instead of soul-searching. Public figures are inclined to look in the direction of the cameras and say with regret, "Television made me do it." People in the media stare back at those in politics and duly note that they just cover what happens and deliver to the public the commercials provided by the politicians.

It is naive to imagine that people in the political realm of their own volition would begin to look beyond the values of television — with their lowest common denominator appeal — in order to present their views in a more thoughtful, detailed manner. But, somehow or other, the contemporary climate needs to change. Suggesting legislation to mandate specific guidelines for political ads provokes stirring defenses of the First Amendment, with its freedom of speech and of the press. Enacting legal measures that would include definite rules for advertising is probably impossible across the board in American political life. However, where public money is used to finance a campaign (on the national, state, and local levels), it certainly can be delivered with some strings attached. For example, the Federal Election Campaign Act (FECA), which established funding procedures for presidential campaigns, could be amended to include language that any candidate receiving public money must personally approve every ad, whether broadcast or print. Moreover, if charges are made about the candidate's opponent, the candidate and his organization would be expected to substantiate the charges for the public, either in the ad itself or in a meeting open to the press and public upon release of the ad.

It would be possible, too, to limit the amount of public money earmarked for television advertising. How about a maximum of one-quarter or one-third of the total amount rather than two-thirds? The redirected money could be spent on information-oriented print ads or direct-mail pieces and grassroots efforts. (In presidential politics, there is the sad irony that the public, through tax dollars, currently pays for the negative ads the same public, in study after study, says it dislikes.) Besides provisions about advertising, acceptance of public money could also mandate participation in a definite number of debates, scheduled at various times during the campaign and methodically spaced out — such as three over the last six weeks before election day.

By linking specific measures to public money, candidates would be directly responsible for *all* messages circulated in their name — the negative as well as the positive — and the candidates would know that they had to take part in a series of planned debates. There would not be the distracting sideshows of "debates over the debates" that now occur frequently. Establishing clear rules on the presidential level is particularly important. The symbolic significance of the presidency is so great in American political life that arguably candidates for other offices would take their cues from those seeking the highest office. In the reverse of Gresham's Law applied to politics, the worthwhile aspects of genuine public policy debates might drive out the poisonously negative elements, changing the environment for both campaigning and governing.

Simplicity is one characteristic of today's political communication. What a public figure says in an ad or as part of a news report competes for people's attention with an ever-increasing number of other messages, delivered via the television, the radio, the computer screen, or on paper. In the world of television, with the multi-channel capability of cable and satellite reception, the zapper reigns. Equipped with a remote control device for rapid channel-changing, the modern viewer (according to television executives) is much less interested in watching entire programs than in watching the tube itself with its diverse possibilities. What will arrest attention for a relatively brief period?

Conceptually, Cable News Network (CNN) and Music Television (MTV) share the common trait of offering their respective audiences the immediate reward of a desired message — up-to-the-minute information or an entertaining tune-video. With so much competition, a fad like "trash TV" is inevitable, as programmers seek to capture viewers by using whatever tactic diverts some people for some time. In fact, the emergence of "trash TV," complete with the freaky repulsiveness of Morton Downey, Jr., and Geraldo Rivera, occurred at the same time as the nasty 1988 presidential campaign. This is not so much a coincidence as a cultural convergence — the larger popular culture intersecting with the political culture, with the values of television influencing the political communication.

Besides being relatively simple, political messages now arrive in such volume and with such velocity that they test the public's attention span. New information keeps replacing yesterday's. This situation contributes to volatility in public thinking, leading to dramatic shifts in survey findings because people lack a certainty of viewpoint. It also affects political and governmental action.

Speed-of-light, global communications create their own environment, where the rush of reaction can overwhelm and crowd out more deliberate reflection and action. In the electoral realm, a charge — especially one delivered in a television ad with wide circulation — demands an immediate countercharge of rebuttal, or the charge (no matter whether legitimate or contrived) will probably stick in the public's mind as an unfavorable characteristic of the candidate. A weakness, among many, of the Dukakis campaign was a hesitancy to respond to the ads of the Bush campaign and of the groups supporting Bush.

Expecting journalism to correct fabrications or distortions is admirable. Unfortunately, it is no longer realistic. A print or broadcast report about an ad appears once, while the ad in question has multiple exposures. A broadcast report that uses visual elements from the ad can, in fact, have the opposite effect from its intended one. The charges in the spot can receive even greater amplification. In 1988, an independent committee supporting the Bush-Quayle ticket produced an ad with a picture of a convicted murderer, Willie Horton, who committed a rape while on furlough from a Massachusetts prison. Dukakis's support of the furlough program was criticized in the spot, which ran primarily on cable television. Network journalists, however, repeatedly used images from the ad in discussing Democratic claims that using the photo of and details about Horton, a black, was racially motivated. The Bush campaign, conveniently, denied direct responsibility, while the Dukakis campaign avoided the subject in its ads. Serious damage, though, had been done.

A year-and-a-half after his defeat in an April 1990 speech before the American Civil Liberties Union of Hawaii, Dukakis stated, "I said in my acceptance speech at Atlanta that the 1988 election was not about ideology, but about competence. I was wrong. It was about *phraseology*. It was about 10-second sound bites. And made-for-TV backdrops. And going negative. I made a lot of mistakes in the '88 campaign, but none was as damaging as my failure to understand this phenomenon, and the need to respond immediately — and effectively — to distortions of one's record and one's positions."

In terms of governance, Jeffrey Tulis explains how different the present is from the nineteenth century. He focuses on Abraham Lincoln and that president's methodical, strategic use of communication with the public.

> Lincoln makes clear not only that he did not lack opportunity [for public statements], but that such opportunities were the problem. Hastily formed statements might engender a course of policy that was unintended. Finally, Lincoln indicates that "silence" will enhance the persuasive power of those speeches that he does deliver. Stressing the need to make his pronouncements on "proper" or authoritative occasions, Lincoln recognizes the need to rest his authority on the Constitution rather than upon raw popular will. For popular will is transient, and may be the object upon which authority might have to be brought to bear.[8]

Today, of course, the conduct of statecraft includes constant measurement of popular will through polling, and journalists covering public figures (from the president on down) seek immediate reactions to events, policy initiatives, or statements. Being accessible and willing to respond are critical attributes for the success of politicians. Given these circumstances, silence is no longer golden, and a "no comment" can provoke additional questions as well as a certain amount of suspicion.

One of the most telling assessments of the consequences of contemporary communications on governance was written by Lloyd Cutler, a Washington attorney, who was White House counsel the last two years of the Carter administration. He discusses in detail how television news affects "the timing and the substance of the policy decisions that an American president is required to make." Cutler discriminates between newspapers and television, noting both the "wider reach and faster impact" of broadcast coverage—"Because TV news accelerates public awareness, the time for response is now even briefer. If an ominous foreign event is featured in TV news [he mentions the Soviet invasion of Afghanistan in 1979 as an example], the president and his advisers feel bound to make a response in time for the next evening news broadcast."[9] The medium itself, especially its visual nature, plays a definite role in the formulation of policy. As Cutler points out, "TV is quintessentially a medium that transmits simple surface impressions, while national policy issues are infinitely complex and many-sided. The ugliness of military combat or economic deprivation can be graphically conveyed in a few pictures and sounds; the complex policy considerations that usually lie behind a decision to risk these consequences are much more difficult to explain."[10] This situation, so different from conditions for governance even three decades ago, means greater linkage between statecraft and stagecraft, with decisions about policy and presentation influencing each other intimately and repeatedly.

As participants in political life and in communications gain greater understanding of their relationship and its varied consequences, is it foolish to ask for less emphasis on quantitative concerns and more concentration on qualitative matters? Of course, the public is phantom, when compared to the democratic ideal celebrated on national holidays. But a majority that is momentary yet decisive in establishing priorities and policies can ultimately result in political life of instant gratification, while the long-term health and maintenance of the total body politic languishes.

Kant encouraged readers of his philosophy, categorically and imperatively, to treat people as ends rather than as means or objects. Those in contemporary public life and in popular communications might do well to think of people as citizens instead of as consumers or, even worse, couch potatoes. Implicit in such an appeal is a respect or dignity that has been sorely missing in recent years. Television values have their place and their reason for being. Democratic values — of an albeit idealistically knowledgeable citizenry exercising deliberate judgment about the most significant civic concerns of a given time — should have their place, too, and they deserve fostering.

5

Cyclops or Big Bird?

The day after Ronald Reagan's landslide re-election in 1984, Walter Mondale emerged from the rubble of his campaign to explain to journalists (and through them to the public at large) why he had not been elected president. The former senator and vice president ticked off several different factors that contributed to his political defeat, but he dwelt on one. "Modern politics today requires a mastery of television," Mondale said. "I've never really warmed up to television and, in fairness to television, it's never warmed up to me." Three months later in a speech to union leaders, Mondale was even more emphatic in blaming television for his defeat. The medium, *not* his political or policy message, was the principal problem, he asserted, adding that what happened was actually a failure in "marketing and packaging" an appealing image.

More objective analysts know that television and other media played a relatively small role in the outcome of the 1984 election. Winning forty-nine states and 59 percent of the total vote, as Reagan did, demonstrated deeply rooted support for continuing what had begun in Reagan's first term. Mondale's interpretation, however, is illustrative of what has become knee-jerk rationalization for electoral losers. It is the messenger's fault, they claim—which means, of course, that the telegenic style of the victor triumphs over the (always) more enlightened substance of the vanquished. Blaming popular forms of communication, especially television, is easy. Increasingly, the small screen has become a large, indeed national, dart board, at which individuals and groups throw their complaints about political and social problems. But coming to a sophisticated understanding of media impact (and television's role in such an equation) is a vastly more complicated undertaking.

An arched eyebrow is the appropriate response to most statements by public figures about the dimensions and implications of popular communications in American political life. These recipients of attention are rarely satisfied with the treatment they receive. (The size of a politician's ego is roughly equivalent to the area he or she represents.) Negative information of whatever kind is perceived as a personal challenge, if not an outright affront. This attitude spans the history of the republic, and biographies of public figures provide what seem to be obligatory outbursts, private or public, about the wayward press. Underlying these statements is the notion that the communications messenger, singularly or collectively, has such considerable power, that the public good (as interpreted by the self-absorbed public figure, of course) is jeopardized or, in some cases, even defeated.

The case of Thomas Jefferson is a telling but representative example. A picture of Jefferson graces the cover of *Speaking of a Free Press*, a booklet published in 1974 by the American Newspaper Publishers Association Foundation. This collection of celebratory quotations carries five ringing endorsements of the press by the man from Monticello, including the one invoked so often by newspaper people: "Were it left to me to decide whether we should have government without newspapers or newspapers without government, I should not hesitate for a moment to prefer the latter. But I should mean that every man should receive those papers and be capable of reading them." Jefferson wrote these words in 1787, when a free press, in theory, seemed an unalloyed advantage to the democratic experiment he was so instrumental in designing. However, governmental experience, notably his eight years as president from 1801 to 1809, tempered the Jeffersonian idealism. In his second inaugural address, delivered March 4, 1805, he takes direct aim at the partisan publications opposing his presidency:

> . . . the artillery of the press has been levelled against us, charged with whatsoever its licentiousness could devise or dare.

> These abuses of an institution so important to freedom and
> science, are deeply to be regretted, inasmuch as they tend to
> lessen its usefulness, and to sap its safety; they might, indeed,
> have been corrected by the wholesome punishments reserved
> and provided by the laws of the several States against false-
> hood and defamation; but public duties more urgent press on
> the time of public servants, and the offenders have therefore
> been left to find their punishment in the public indignation.[1]

In this formal and official expression, the criticism is measured
—"the inestimable liberty of the press and its demoralizing li-
centiousness" coexist, with the effects of the abuses both real and
regrettable. Two years later, in a private letter, Jefferson assumes
what today might be called a Nixonian stance via-à-vis the press.
His abstract admiration of a free press has withered.

> It is a melancholy truth, that a suppression of the press could
> not more completely deprive the nation of its benefits, than
> is done by its abandoned prostitution to falsehood. Nothing
> can now be believed which is seen in a newspaper. Truth itself
> becomes suspicious by being put into that polluted vehicle. The
> real extent of this state of misinformation is known only to those
> who are in situations to confront facts within their knowledge
> with the lies of the day. I really look with commiseration over
> the great body of my fellow citizens, who, reading newspapers,
> live and die in the belief, that they have known something of
> what has been passing in the world in their time. . . .[2]

Public figures, such as Jefferson, are incapable of offering a
fair, complete, and accurate appraisal of the messages of political communication or the impact of popular communications
on political life. As the principal actors in the continuing drama
of statecraft, these people need to perform in public, which means
largely through the media. Thus they conduct several different
moves depending on the situation. Sometimes the public figures
and journalists work closely together in what biology teachers
call a state of symbiosis. At other times, there is hostility and an
adversarial relationship. Frequently there is a convergence of the
two, resulting in a like-dislike professional arrangement similar
to a love-hate relationship. In all cases the viewpoint of the public figure is clouded by subjective reactions. They shift blame instead of analyze, with the ultimate intention of offering "the other

side" for the sake of greater historical understanding and, in some cases, sympathy. Such impressions about the consequences of communication are interesting, but imprecise.

A meaningful survey of media impact requires looking away from the statements of those engaged in statecraft. Assessing media consequence has become the contemporary preoccupation of political scientists, sociologists, historians, communications scholars, and journalists. As Michael J. Robinson, himself a political scientist and talented media watcher, said, "For the last dozen years, the media have been to campaign 'theory' what sex has been to clinical psychiatry—the first and foremost factor analyzed."[3]

This fascination persists into the 1990s, with analysis of the media by academics and journalists becoming a growth industry. In presidential politics alone, the seemingly endless campaign conducted between elections involves not only aspirants in hot pursuit of contributions and news coverage to enhance their positions for candidacy. It also includes a multiplying number of media monitors who look back at each campaign, attempting to decipher the meaning and significance of the journalistic coverage and advertisements.

A principal reason for the outpouring of books and articles, not to mention the prevalence of post-mortem conferences and symposia, is the lack of consensus about what conclusive, definitive effects the media have in electing a president. That the popular forms of communication, particularly television, have changed the ways campaigns are waged is a cliché of political discourse today. Candidates, indeed most public figures, conduct themselves with the media's power of projection as a primary consideration. Noting this obvious consequence of media involvement is one thing; determining with precision and certitude the effects of the media on the public and our political life in general is another, more problematic matter. Are the media, in effect, power brokers, possessing Cyclopean influence of immense strength? Or are they educators who do not mind being entertaining to lighten the instructional load—in essence, a flock of Big Birds, performing not too far from "Sesame Street"? These questions, on opposite ends of the spectrum of communications power, frame the current debate, and trying to answer them has created a medium-size library of analyses, where conflicting, even contradictory, conclusions abound.

To illustrate how difficult it is to resolve definitively the media power debate, all one has to do is consider some specific passages in two books by two of the more respected observers of American political life, James David Barber, the political scientist, and Theodore H. White, the influential political journalist and author. Both offer descriptive, historical accounts of presidential politics, especially the growing prominence of popular communications as messengers about public figures and public affairs. Both, however, muddy rather than clarify fundamental questions related to the exact consequences of the media in our political life.

Early in his *The Pulse of Politics*, Barber calls the political reporter of today a "middleman . . . the new power-broker, filling the gap vacated by yesterday's [party] bosses."

> There he stands, between people and President. Whether he knows it or not, the impressions he composes and conveys are now the blood of Presidential politics. The journalistic tyros of old — the Hearsts and Luces and Murrows, whose impact on politics was often personal and direct — are gone. The collective, loose-jointed journalistic fraternity of today is all the more powerful because its influence is pervasive and indirect and atmospheric, an element of the cultural air we breathe.[4]

In the concluding chapter, he invests the "middleman" journalist with even greater significance. The power is no longer "indirect"; it is strikingly direct and formidable. He portrays journalists as the new "storytellers," the shapers of the myths and tales that used to be the province of literary artists and intellectuals.

> Yet in fact we depend, far more profoundly than we have realized, on storytellers to pluck from the chaos of experience the plot of the next adventure. From the beginning, even geography had to give way to the force of myth: Columbus, flying in the face of the science of his day, believing instead in Marco Polo's tales of the Indies, the Puritans, aiming for Virginia and hitting Cape Cod, sustained by the vision of a New Zion, on down to the wildly improbable but mythically compelling idea of putting a man on the moon. The pictures in our heads conquered the ground beneath our feet. The painters of those pic-

tures, when they can get them believed, exercise a power that
is nothing less than the power to set a course of civilization.
In modern politics, lacking grander visions, we make do with
glimpses of possibility and shades of meaning — a kaleidoscope
of fact and metaphor and judgment. Journalism, our composite
Homer, delivers those partial sightings, which substitute for
heroic myth. If it is the default of the political parties that
burdens journalism with sorting out candidates, it is the default of the contemporary intellectuals that leaves to journalists the task of composing our ruling ideas.[5]

There is a certain element of restraint in Barber's language.
He qualifies his conclusions by using such phrases as "substitute
for heroic myth," "the default of the political parties," and "the
default of the contemporary intellectuals." But this hedging does
not adequately resolve the book's internal contradictions about
the precise consequences of mass-mediated political communication. Influence that is "pervasive and indirect and atmospheric"
is less substantial, less meaningful, than "the power to set a course
of civilization" or the ability "of sorting out candidates" or "composing our ruling ideas."

In addition to the analytical inconsistencies, Barber's generalizations about the role of the media vis-à-vis candidates and ideas
are debatable. Specific circumstances are critical — the particular politicians involved, the effectiveness of campaigning, the
mood of the public, what is actually happening at home and
abroad. How these factors intersect and become known through
the different forms of communication will vary from election to
election. The "sorting out" process is vastly complex. Moreover,
in the rarefied air of "ruling ideas," journalists play a part in *presenting* such thoughts to the nation, but that is quite different
from "composing" them. During the eight years of the Reagan
presidency, the "ruling ideas" of American political life moved
decidedly rightward, yet conservatives continued to rail against
the liberal media and its leftward slant. The ideas that mattered
came from academics, intellectuals, and policy thinkers at uni-
versities and research centers, such as Stanford University's Hoover
Institution, the Heritage Foundation, and the American Enterprise Institute — not from the journalists.

Trying to resolve questions of media impact is even more diffi-

cult for White in *America in Search of Itself.* This book, the
author's last in his "making of the president" series, includes his
reminiscences and conclusions about presidential politics since
1956, when he began to follow and write about campaigns for
the White House as his principal vocation. Throughout the book,
White argues that television is a dominant — if not *the* dominant
— force in national elections. The title of one chapter is "The
Reign of Television," and in that chapter he offers his opinion
about the medium:

> Television in modern politics has been as revolutionary as the
> development of printing in the time of Gutenberg. Once Guten-
> berg put the Bible in print, and others followed to explain the
> world to those who could read, neither church nor prince could
> maintain authority without controlling, or yielding to, the word
> in print. Television, especially in America, explains the world
> to those who, if they will not read, can look.[6]

Each time White refers to television he uses such charged language. However, in the end, he is only partially persuasive — and
accurate — in stating his case. The impact of television is more
complicated, less of a black-and-white condition, and failure to
come to terms with this complexity leads to a puzzling, indeed
paradoxical, contradiction.

Certainly, White is correct in noting that television has become "the central arena of American politics." Presidential candidates do devise their daily schedules to penetrate as many "areas
of dominant influence"— the major television centers or media
markets — as they can, and more than half of their campaign
money goes to the production and airing of the television commercials. To report that television has "become the atmosphere
of politics in which politicians breathed or suffocated to death"
is one thing. To deduce impressionistically from these facts that
voters now "judge the rivals for leadership through the slit that
television offers them as an eye piece" seems too large a claim,
as does White's remark that "the networks control the nation's
imagination." These assertions lack the necessary proof that would
invest them with genuine meaning. Television might "reign" over
the candidates, dictating scheduling and the spending of campaign funds, yet to say television is sovereign vis-à-vis the public

and the formation of public opinion exaggerates the situation and is not verifiable. Other factors — personal values, family contacts, party or individual loyalties — enter into the process of judging public figures. The "slit" of television is *not* the only way of seeing political life.

White's attempt to explain the impact of television and its relationship to the influence of events, ideas, or conditions occurring within the society as a whole is even more contradictory — and less satisfactory. In his view, "it is television which is reality," and he goes so far as to say: "In a national election . . . Americans would vote as the producers of television unveiled reality for them." Statements like these put the medium before the message. Such generalizations are vulnerable to criticism, and White himself seems to back off from such claims when confronted by events of genuine national significance. For example, he devotes considerable attention to the Iranian hostage crisis of 1979 and 1980 and to the economic problems of that time. These occurrences — realities, if you will — had profound consequences on Jimmy Carter and his re-election effort.

At one point White writes of Carter:

> There could have been no Carter presidency without tele-
> vision. But he who comes to power by television must be pre-
> pared to be destroyed by television. For the men and women
> of television, however hungry for drama and clash in politics,
> are compelled to report the larger drama of upheaval, change,
> and erosions of old faiths. Carter was to be undermined not
> by the malice of television, or by the superior skills of the Rea-
> gan television team in 1980, but by history itself. Television,
> on its morning and evening news, would show a world Amer-
> ica could no longer control.[7]

In this paragraph, "history itself"— reality *and* the messages about it — dominate the medium. Television transmits the "upheaval, change, and erosions of old faiths." Later, near the end of the book, White reinforces his view that political and social realities determined the election of 1980. The substance of Reagan and all that he represented proved more compelling and attractive than the substance of Carter. Style with its telegenic images was subordinate: "There is no escaping the stark fact of the repudiation, in the election of 1980, of a regime that had outlived its time, and though the personalities of the candidates played a vital role, ideas, and the programs that flow from these ideas, are more important."[8]

Recognizing the tricky nature of making conclusions about the consequences of communications is, of course, not new. In a cogent treatment of the evolution of concern about the effects of popular communications that really began in 1922 with the publication of Walter Lippmann's *Public Opinion*, Bernard Berelson says, "Some kinds of *communication* on some kinds of *issues*, brought to the attention of some kinds of *people* under some kinds of *conditions*, have some kinds of effects."[9] That statement, so strategically worded, might not take someone very far in isolating specific, identifiable consequences; however, it does raise appropriate cautionary flags. Each element requires analysis. Impact can easily vary from situation to situation, from one time to another. Any "last words" on the subject should be written in pencil.

In the 1940s, political scientists and sociologists began detailed, empirical studies of public attitudes and political behavior to try to better understand the relationship between the different types of media and representative citizens. The landmark study of the 1940 presidential campaign between Franklin Roosevelt and Wendell Willkie appeared in its complete and academic edition in 1948 as *The People's Choice: How the Voter Makes Up His Mind in a Presidential Election.*[10]

In this study the conclusions of Bernard Berelson, Paul Lazarsfeld, and Hazel Gaudet stood in stark juxtaposition to earlier, less scientifically sophisticated claims of substantial media power. Instead of the instruments of communication operating like a hypodermic injection on the body politic in America, with immediate and direct results on the nation's collective bloodstream as was previously claimed, what really happened was more like the workings of an eye-dropper—an incremental process with cumulative effects over time. From the 1940s well into the 1960s, analysts found that media effects were limited and interpersonal communication was actually more influential than messages coming from mass media sources. "Ideas often flow *from* radio and print *to* the opinion leaders and *from* them to the less active sec-tions of the population." This phenomenon became known as the "two-step flow of communication," and as a concept it helped shape serious discussions of the impact of the media for almost twenty years.

Since the 1960s, however, the pendulum has swung away from a position of minimal, indirect consequence to a place between the two extremes of considerable or minimal power. Historical events, cultural circumstances, and technological innovations converged in the 1960s to change the ways many people evaluated the effects of mass communications on the public.

Although Edward R. Murrow and other broadcast journalists demonstrated the promise and possibilities of television news during the 1950s, the medium as a source of reporting about current affairs came of age in the 1960s. One year, 1963, stands out as being critically significant. Two of the networks, CBS and NBC, began airing half-hour evening broadcasts in September of that year, and all three networks devoted blanket coverage to the assassination and burial of President John Kennedy in November 1963. The shooting of the assassin, Lee Harvey Oswald, live on screen stunningly dramatized the immediacy and impact of television. For four days, the nation rarely blinked. Late that same year, the Roper Organization conducted one of its periodic surveys of public attitudes toward the mass media. In two previous surveys (completed in 1959 and 1962) newspapers led all other media as the primary source of news. In 1963, television replaced newspapers as the dominant medium for news, a situation that has become much more pronounced in recent years. (The difference between television and newspapers in 1963 was 2 percent. Today the spread is about 30 percent.)

Since the 1970s, another concept has been explored by social scientists and communication scholars—"the agenda-setting function" of the mass media. Bernard Cohen gave attention to this phenomenon a decade earlier, "the press is significantly more than a purveyor of information and opinion. It may not be successful much of the time in telling people what to think, but it is stunningly successful in telling its readers what to think *about*."[11] What the public reads, sees, and hears *can* (not necessarily *will*) be a factor in understanding or forming an opinion about a figure or issue. In electoral politics today, receiving attention is a fundamental concern. Without media exposure a potential candidate remains largely unknown — in effect, a non-person politically. Gaining some kind of attention — being on the public's agenda — is the necessary first step the potential candidate must take; however, voters might ultimately reject the figure for nomination or for office.

In *Behind the Front Page: A Candid Look at How the News Is Made*, David Broder notes that with journalists, "our values control our most important daily decisions: what to put in and what to leave out. Those judgments are inescapable because of time and space, of which there is never enough to tell the whole story." Those "daily decisions," involving professional as well as subjective criteria, do have impact and deserve probing. Out of a large field of candidates seeking, say, a party's presidential nomination, which ones receive coverage? How much coverage? What kind of coverage? Finding answers to these questions is important, but — once again — being discriminating in drawing conclusions is essential.

Shortly before he withdrew from the multi-candidate race to be the Democratic presidential candidate in 1988, Bruce Babbitt remarked with good-natured exaggeration: "I would like to say a word to all of those Americans who worry that the press is a giant conspiracy that controls politics: You have nothing to fear. The press has little or no influence." Babbitt had, indeed, been the beneficiary of enthusiastically positive treatment in early 1988 — one newspaper referred to him as the "darling of the presidential campaign press corps"— but the coverage had virtually no impact in broadening his support in the first electoral tests. He left the race two days after the New Hampshire primary.

Although it is refreshingly untypical for a losing politician *not* to find some fault with the media, Babbitt is more playful than pertinent in describing the influence of popular communications in politics. He, of course, is partially correct in implying that "the press" cannot by themselves create the type of voting allegiance needed to win a major elective contest. Other factors (such as prior candidate knowledge or loyalty as well as opponent dissatisfaction or dislike) play definite roles.

While the media can focus attention on a subject, put it on the agenda, it does seem more influential in shaping opinion in a negative way than in a positive, support-building manner. In other words, amplification of what might be construed as damaging or even ambiguous information tends to be treated more seriously by the public, leading to questions and doubts. It is easier for the influence to be destructive than to be constructive.

The experiences of Gary Hart in both 1984 and 1988 illustrate this point. In his first try for the Democratic presidential nomination, the Colorado senator's upset win in the New Hampshire primary created a flood of publicity, which in less than a week's time took a relative unknown and turned him into Walter Mondale's most serious challenger. The media certainly made the public *think about* the candidate of "new ideas," and there was a fad-like fascination for several days. However, when Mondale regained his footing and began to mock his opponent's less-than-detailed abstractions by asking, "Where's the beef?" Hart could not translate the favorable print and broadcast attention into the support he needed. By contrast, the disclosures about his personal life in 1987 quickly removed him from serious contention for the 1988 nomination. The negative information, delivered in the bold, breathless style reserved for scandal, made a viable candidacy impossible. Were the media the decisive factors in both cases? Certainly not. Was the amplification of news in 1987 of greater consequence than in 1984? It would be difficult to think otherwise.

Studies to discover the specific effects of popular forms of political communication have been taking place during a period marked by growth in the public's media usage, especially the watching of television, and by the decline of institutions involved in the formation of political opinions, notably the two major parties. These phenomena — as well as the introduction of new methodological approaches — have drawn into question such concepts as the "two-step flow of communication." Interpersonal contacts no longer seem as important. Increasingly, people in their homes or apartments receive political information through news reports or advertisements on television. They might not seek out this kind of information on their own, but it is delivered to them as part of what arrives over the airwaves. At the same time the electorate has become more independent and less inclined to take cues from "opinion leaders" — party bosses, union chieftains, business executives, and the like. Given the new media and political environment, the "two-step flow of communication" (figure 1) now looks simplistic and anachronistic.

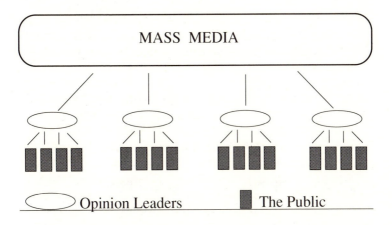

MASS MEDIA

Opinion Leaders   ■ The Public

The current conditions and circumstances demand a more complex diagram, one that takes into account *both* popular forms of communication and interpersonal exchange. Since all communication is a flowing, dynamic process, any schema should also indicate that fluidity. (See figure 2.)

Finding a new way of describing the interrelationship between political communication and opinion formation is just one dimension to more comprehensive understanding of media impact. It is also important to try to isolate and explain specific effects occurring within our changing political-communications environment. Verification — either empirically or historically — is critical. One of the most successful attempts is *Press, Party, and Presidency* by Richard Rubin. After briefly delineating how these three institutions have operated with respect to each other since the time of Washington and Jefferson, Rubin focuses on the twentieth century. He identifies Theodore Roosevelt as the "first modern 'media' president," noting that Roosevelt's masterful manipulation of communications was instrumental in the "*disengagement* of the president from the party." Over time this led to the decline of party rule in presidential politics, with the disengagement becoming markedly more pronounced when television began to devote greater attention to the presidential selection process.

Seeing the press, national political parties, and the president as competitors in channeling public opinion, Rubin explains that in recent years there has been a weakening of both the party struc-

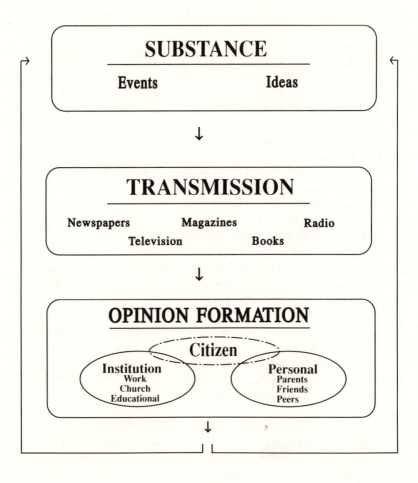

ture and of the presidency. Concurrently, there has been growth in the impact and influence of the media. He is careful, however, in explaining the actual effects of the media. He acknowledges that many public figures believe the media have enormous power, the conclusive say about someone's ultimate success or failure. Such an opinion might be comforting for politicians seeking scapegoats, but it is neither verifiable nor justifiable in the total context of the environment that currently exists. The situation is more involved and complex because of (in Rubin's phrase) "the limitations of social science research" and the imprecise methods available to measure specific, individual effects. Still, Rubin tries to be as definite as possible in dealing with the media power debate: "Individual responses to media messages, i.e., their micro-effects, may be presently small and hard to sort out with the tools we have. But the *indirect* influence of television on our key electoral institutions, i.e., its macro-effects, are already large, measurable, and crucial in reshaping, rechanneling, and reorganizing American political power."[12]

In other words, while social science and behavioral researchers wrestle with the design of studies they hope will eventually lead to more definite conclusions about the "micro-effects" of the media on the electorate, the political strategists and people working in communications have already altered what they do to accommodate and to emphasize the media's role in politics. These "macro-effects"—such as committing more campaign money to broadcast "air time," designing schedules to penetrate major media markets at strategic times, and conducting convention proceedings to be most flattering to the ticket and party—are readily identifiable changes within our system accentuating media involvement. Discriminating between individual and institutional impact helps reduce potential confusion and misunderstanding.

At a time when the volume of mass-mediated messages about politics as well as their velocity have increased sharply, it is possible to see our contemporary political life with greater clarity. To elaborate on the phenomenon of agenda-setting: The volume and velocity of information make it more possible than ever before to acquaint a person with public figures and issues, but this does not mean that the person's attitudes or behavior will be ap-

preciably affected. Pervasiveness does *not* automatically translate into power. The similarity between "omnipresence" and "om-
nipotence" ends at the prefix the two words share.

However, another dimension to agenda-setting in the Age of
Personality is the circumstance that the intense focus on the individual personality of the president or those-who-would-be president places a strong, almost stationary spotlight on the presidency
as an institution. This means that Congress and the Judiciary
might be constitutionally co-equal branches, but they are not
really of that stature in the mind of the mass public, which learns
about governmental activity through the popular forms of communication on a regular (if not daily) basis.

The difficulty of measuring the precise effects of communications on individuals is compounded by the variable nature of potential impact. No two elections are exactly alike. Different circumstances dictate different consequences. However, there may
be a general rule: the greater the public uncertainty, the greater
the possibility of media influence. Political scientist Thomas E.
Patterson called his study of the 1976 presidential contest *The
Mass Media Election*. Neither the appointed president Gerald
Ford nor the relatively unknown Jimmy Carter had the deep electoral support that comes from long-term exposure and service.
This allowed the media to play a more significant role in the selection process. Patterson takes aim at the popular impression
that television exerts greater influence than other media in the
realm of presidential politics. His elaborate survey research proved
that newspaper coverage in 1976 had more definite impact on
the public than television coverage.[13] Although politicians seemingly live and campaign for the klieg lights and the mini-cams,
in this instance television — instead of acting as a Cyclops with
overwhelming power to affect voters' behavior — was closer to being the Greek chorus of the campaign. However, one event reflected substantial television influence. Immediately after the debate in which Ford (prematurely, as it turns out) said "there is
no Soviet domination of Eastern Europe," a poll reported that
Ford had done a better job by 44 to 43 percent. The next day —
following numerous television replays of the gaffe and print and
broadcast commentary — Carter was the public choice by 62 to

17 percent, a stunning reversal. This is an illustration of the consequences of communications amplification, but it is dangerous to carry such findings too far. Context remains critical.

Four years later, the circumstances had changed dramatically. By 1980, Carter had established himself (for good or ill) in the public mind, and his opponent, Ronald Reagan, was similarly established for the electorate to consider. According to political journalist and media critic Jeff Greenfield, "*television and the media made almost no difference in the outcome of the 1980 Presidential campaign.*"[14] "The real campaign" was shaped and influenced by fundamental political realities. In his treatment of Reagan, Greenfield acknowledges that in the eyes of many people, including several influential journalists, the former actor's political ascent was the apotheosis of media politics. These people, seduced by the allure of theatrics and celebrity, think that scripted lines gracefully delivered substitute for substantive policy proposals. Again and again, Greenfield takes issue with this image-is-everything notion. Stagecraft is important, to be sure, but statecraft — political thinking and action — animates political performance.

In the case of 1980, Reagan's ideology, which had remained consistent for over twenty years, finally appealed to a large enough political base to win the nomination and election. His media skills were, of course, considerable; he *seemed* more presidential than the incumbent president. But his political ideas and stands proved more significant to his success. As Greenfield states, "The aspects of a genuine 'media' candidate — carefully controlled, measured answers to questions, an ability to project calm, unruffled emotions in the presence of difficulties or hostile questions, doling out responses to questions with computerlike regularity, avoiding controversy and trouble — these were not the skills of Ronald Reagan as he campaigned for the Republican nomination, nor when he battled Jimmy Carter for the Presidency." Several of the statements Reagan made in 1980 were hopelessly uninformed — his remarks that trees were serious pollutants and that the Soviet people were at times reduced to eating sawdust stand out — yet voters were willing to forgive (if not forget) such lapses. Why? People knew what Reagan stood for — he represented more than just an image — and they were willing to see if he could reduce the size and cost of the federal government, ease the regulations of business and industry, and restore the military to a stature where it could avoid intimidation from other countries, large and small.

In contrast to Reagan, Carter was perceived by the citizenry as a political figure without a coherent set of principles. He operated for one term without a definable political theme, let alone an identifiable ideology, and he could not project through the media more than the impression of someone who was sincere and hardworking. Carter had difficulty summoning genuine support because his message was so muddled and contradictory. The media reported whatever he said or proposed, but the lack of a theme produced confusion, also dutifully noted by journalists. Carter's difficulties, including the haunting economic problems and the Iranian hostage crisis, were ultimately political conditions of greater consequence than the involvement of the media in the 1980 campaign.

The variability of media influence in today's presidential politics is also prevalent throughout the rest of American political life, making it impossible to offer chiseled tablets of definite, justifiable, and enduring statements. At the presidential level, this situation will remain constant — and controversial — as long as the current electoral process exists. The media have become central to campaigns because politicians and their strategists have decided that the new rules for winning require communication primarily through broadcast outlets and the press. The media, in search of dramatic stories as well as advertising revenue, have been more than willing to be the political messengers, resulting in a situation of mutual manipulation. Such interplay will be circumstance-dependent, yielding variable results and effects. A communications Cyclops of robust influence is, one deduces, a very distant possibility — but so too is the opposite analogy, the kinder and gentler Big Bird, who offers an occasional lesson as well as diverting entertainment.

Instead of looking at the consequences of political communication in terms of mythical polarities, it might be more instructive to focus on another metaphor. The political-media environment is subject to climatic changes, with effects on those who make and inhabit that environment. The different forms of communication surround us with political information of one kind or another in a fairly constant manner. This information can pop up unexpectedly as we watch television or listen to the radio, or we can experience it more deliberately by reading newspapers and magazines. On a day-to-day basis, the effects of such exposure are gradual or cumulative—akin to a tan. At some times, however, when environmental conditions change dramatically, the result can be a tornado, hurricane, or blizzard. These are jolting blasts with immediate and substantial repercussions that reverberate throughout the environment, affecting institutions and individuals alike. These occasions—such as the revelations about Gary Hart or John Tower—strike with a different force and produce different kinds of consequences.

Generalizations, like stereotypes, make it easier to see complexity, but they take a watcher of statecraft and stagecraft just so far. Knowing the existing climate and circumstances in depth is the real first step to understanding the impact of popular communications on our political life.

6
Temptations of Technology

One of the paradoxes of the communications revolution that has been taking place during the second half of the twentieth century is the disparity of accomplishment between the creators and the users of this new technology. Engineers and design specialists have produced a communications cornucopia. Satellites circling earth supply speed-of-light transmission of words and pictures throughout the global village. Cable and fiber optic systems make possible interactive television and an array of other participatory networks. Computers of varying sizes and degrees of performance provide rapid data processing and dissemination. However, along with this cornucopia — the preceding examples barely scratch the surface — comes what thus far has been a conundrum for those engaged in American political life.

How do political-governmental figures, people in communications, and the public at large use this wondrous technology most effectively and responsibly? Creating sophisticated, state-of-the-art hardware is one thing. Designing comparably advanced (for lack of a more precise word) software — the actual substance of communications in many respects — is another matter of equal or even greater significance. Finding appropriate and proper uses for the new technology, while avoiding the temptations this technology offers, will be a continuing challenge in the 1990s. And the decisions made during this decade will, ultimately, dictate the direction our political life takes in the twenty-first century.

Television is a medium highly dependent on engaging pictures. There is a visual imperative, and the new, sophisticated technology enhances this dimension. For example, "mini-cams" are highly portable and allow those in television to go almost anywhere to cover public figures in, to use the promotional phrase of one network, "an up-close and personal way." (Again, the emphasis on personality.) In addition, satellites now transmit more pictures at amazing speed, resulting in greater availability of material, both taped and live. More aspects of our political process are available for the public to witness, which is beneficial. But frequently, of course, the most visually compelling taped footage ends up on our television screen at the expense of what might be more substantively nourishing. Similarly, the capability of doing live reports offers a "you-are-there" immediacy to coverage, enabling the viewer at home to watch those in public life carry out some of their duties or interact with reporters. It is of civic value to see a State of the Union speech, a presidential press conference, a congressional committee hearing, or a keynote address at a party convention.

Increasingly, though, since the technology "to go live" exists in such abundance, there is a strong temptation to use it just because it is available. Moreover, the equipment costs so much to buy that usage is given priority to justify the expense of the investment. Possessing the new technology becomes significant in itself and the focus of promotional campaigns to secure more viewers and higher ratings. (Pity the local station that does not have a satellite van these days.)

However, especially on the local level and during the frenzy of a campaign, little substantive preparation precedes live-yet-remote telecasts. Reporters thrust microphones into the faces of candidates and ask questions of such enduring significance as: How is your campaign going? What do you think of the latest polls? Do you expect to win? Most politicians are more than happy to deliver messages to the citizenry in formats without editing. These public figures have more control in such situations. Even when probing questions are posed, they can be evaded more easily in live encounters of limited duration.

In *The Great American Video Game*, Martin Schram assesses

the use of satellite technology in the coverage of the 1984 presidential campaign. He notes:

> The compulsion for filling the air with live remote coverage is most often an abdication of the sort of advance planning and constructive editing that produces pieces that are clear and to the point — or at least make a point. In live broadcasting there can be no editing — and often there is not much more thought and planning — to the reports that are aired. Many are, at best, a waste of precious airtime; and at worst, they can be misleading and just plain wrong.[1]

There has been more usage of the live-shot technology since 1984, and the temptations to use it multiply. The electorate gains by "being there," but this experience can come with a cost attached to it. Politicians are able to make statements without challenge or scrutiny. A charge about an opponent can receive amplification that is only modified or corrected in a subsequent broadcast. How many viewers of the original charge will see the other candidate's response?

Modern communications reduce the distance between political life and the public. Virtually every household in America has at least one television set, making it possible for the vast majority of citizens to view (through the prism of TV) the conduct of political life in all of its diversity. The networks cover major occurrences — a presidential speech, a particularly significant congressional investigation, a debate between candidates for national office — while the two channels of the Cable-Satellite Public Affairs Network (C-SPAN) carry proceedings of both the House of Representatives and the Senate. In addition, local and community access cable stations bring activities of municipal, regional, and in some cases state government to citizens of "the wired nation." The actual number of citizens who regularly follow political life by watching such sources is not the issue here. The proliferation of these sources in recent years and their potential for usage in the future are significant concerns that deserve probing.

These forms of media and related instruments of communication are considerably more than high-tech delivery systems for public figures to utilize in relaying their words and actions. The new technology also creates a process of continuing interaction between those in public life and the public at large that makes the concept of "passive reception" of political information obsolete. There are more opportunities now than ever before to participate in different kinds of call-in programs, whether on radio or television, that link public figures with citizens who have questions or comments. These types of programs can be, from time to time, curiously amusing— as conspiracy theorists from left-field or right-field offer their views with the certainty of an umpire who is not always right but never in doubt. Most frequently, however, these discussions focus on more central, mainstream concerns, such as the status of pending legislation or the operations of specific governmental departments.

Mediated exchanges of this kind can be informative to the public figure, to the citizen participating in the program, and to the wider public that is tuned in. The communications technology being used expands the potential of citizen involvement, and it is much easier "to attend" such a forum by staying at home than by traveling across town, or to the state capital, or even to Washington, D.C. In many respects, space and time shrink, while people in political life, policies, and issues become more immediate to those interested enough to take the time to watch, listen, or call.

As beneficial as the intelligent use of modern, interactive communications technology might be, the same instruments can also have questionable consequences in the way such formats handle and deliver political information. Again, as with the desire in television to deploy live-shot equipment, one wonders how much thought precedes the treatment of topics that have political and governmental dimensions. One particularly dubious interactive format is the radio talk-show. In the late 1980s, many of these programs turned up both the heat and the volume in discussing public figures and issues. Especially in large metropolitan areas where a radio station battles for its niche in an environment of narrowcasting, polite conversation between host and caller has often given way to full-throated outbursts. Civil, public discourse gets drowned out by crude shouting matches that appeal to a listener's emotions rather than to anyone's intellect. (Trash TV and Raucous Radio share a common cultural parentage, polluting the airwaves in similar ways.)

A dramatic example of the impact of the high-tech talk-show took place early in 1989, when Congress considered a pay increase for members of the House and Senate, federal officials, and judges. It is legitimate to debate the merits of such an increase and to criticize the procedures used, but what happened — with the involvement of the talk-shows — was distinctly different from any debate of reasoned, pro-con discussion. For the first time in history, forty to fifty local hosts created an informal national network flatly opposed to the salary hike.

Modern technology — radio stations linked together via phone lines and satellite transmissions — enabled the talk-show personalities to call their counterparts in other regions of the country to report — on the air, of course — about support and activities against the measure. Those callers favoring the raise were frequently cut-off or informed they had the intelligence of a hockey puck. In a matter of days, given the intensity of focus and the immediacy of the issue, public opinion crystallized against the hike. (Some surveys reported 85 percent of Americans opposed.) Tea bags jammed the postal system to Washington as the hosts urged people to take part in a 1989 version of the Boston Tea Party. The fax machine in the office of Speaker of the House Jim Wright received messages on a non-stop basis after one radio personage obtained the number and circulated it to others in the new, single-interest network. When it came time for a Congressional decision in early February, all but forty-eight members of the House and six senators voted against the raise.

After the proposal was defeated, several print and broadcast sources devoted reports to the role played by the radio talk-shows in government's handling of this issue. Clearly, something new and different was happening, and the potential for recurrence was ominously obvious. Indeed, several of the self-described "radio activists" said they planned to meet periodically to discuss other political and social topics they deemed worthy of joint amplification. One piece of journalistic analysis (in the *New York Times*) asked: "Is government-by-talk-show the wave of the future?"

The question makes one pause. Such a prospect is not only uninviting but frightening. This new phenomenon, a product of modern communications technology, is a direct challenge to some of our fundamental democratic values. A hallmark of the American political tradition has been deliberate action by duly elected representatives. By explicit design government is a slow-moving vehicle. For instance, *The Federalist Papers* caution against "unqualified compliance with every sudden breeze of passion." The Founders' system established separate branches, staggered terms, countervailing check and balances — with state and local governmental operations following similar patterns in most cases. Such a methodical — albeit on occasion frustrating — structure kept momentary passions at bay; there was greater chance to lower the heat to locate the light.

The threat that comes from the "sudden breeze of passion" has been a subject of worry since our republican democracy was created. The most eloquent commentator on the dangers that can result from a quickly assembled, *ad hoc* mass in the United States is Alexis de Tocqueville. After touring America in the 1830s, he returned to his native France to write *Democracy in America.* Although Tocqueville found much to praise in this fledgling yet self-confident nation, he warned of what he saw as the potential for a "tyranny of the majority." Noting that "public opinion is the dominant power" in this country, he argued that a vocal mob could tyrannically drown out other voices, stifle legitimate dissent, and force political action without the leaden-footed but laudatory deliberateness to decision-making that our governmental system tries to insure. As he notes at one point, "The majority in the United States takes over the business of supplying the individual with a quantity of ready-made opinions and so relieves him of the necessity of forming his own. So there are many theories of philosophy, morality, and politics which everyone adopts unexamined on the faith of public opinion."

Today, over 150 years since Tocqueville offered his warning, the threat that stems from a "tyranny of the majority" still exists. Making that fear even more real are the new, sophisticated forms of communication that create, in effect, a national nervous system. A controversial subject — frequently originating in the body politic, such as the pay raise — stimulates this nervous system and takes on so much urgency that it seems to demand a speedy resolution. The dangers of a "tyranny of the majority" grow when one contemplates the possibilities of what might be called the "tyranny of technology."

As informing and illuminating as instantaneous communication can be, there are political perils in the irresponsible use of this technology. The immediacy, intensity, and impact of these instruments make it difficult for passions of the moment, noble or questionable, to be tempered by time. The contemporary communications environment accelerates and amplifies debate and argument to such a degree that actions might be taken before all sides are investigated. Indeed, in listening to these talk shows, one is stunned to hear so much erroneous information circulate as fact, never to be corrected. Such misinformation is a civic virus, comparable in its way to the phenomenon of a computer virus. With the twin possibility of a "tyranny of the majority" and a "tyranny of technology" present, the risk exists that what has traditionally been our democratic smokehouse — where ideas and proposals were intended to be cured over weeks and months — will become more like a pressure cooker, constantly whistling and frequently exploding.

In considering the question, "Is government-by-talk-show the wave of the future?" a sobering remark of radio and television news pioneer and patron saint Edward R. Murrow bears repeating: "The fact that your voice is amplified to the degree where it reaches from one end of the country to the other does not confer upon you greater wisdom or understanding than you possessed when your voice reached only from one end of the bar to the other." A communicator's concern for creating a cause — and catering to an audience — can cloud thought about civic responsibility and consequence. And, it is legitimate to ask, whither public discourse at a time when ratings mean more than civility?

Public figures have the responsibility of governing, despite the pressure or cries for immediate action delivered by modern communications technology. Being responsive is one thing. Being cornered by a mob is quite another. Continuous reaction to outside stimuli from a momentary majority can lead to a condition resembling St. Vitus's Dance for our body politic. Given the new communications and political environment, it becomes the obligation of those in the media and in public life to keep fundamental, traditional principles of the American democratic order firmly in their thinking as they make decisions about how to use and to respond to the different instruments of popular communication.

The technological here-and-now is troubling enough to those who compare the work of the Constitutional framers with what is happening now in American political life. However, even more extensive usage of live satellite reports in television news or more sophisticated networking of interactive radio programs pale in significance to some of the other temptations of technology that loom on the horizon. Two popular futurologists, Alvin Toffler and John Naisbitt, foretell a new political world in sharp contrast to our past. In *The Third Wave*, Toffler notes, "For the old communication limitations no longer stand in the way of expanded direct democracy. Spectacular advances in communications technology open, for the first time, a mind-boggling array of possibilities for direct citizen participation in political decision-making."[2] For Toffler, "the old objections to direct democracy are growing weaker at precisely the time that the objections to representative democracy are growing stronger."[3]

In *Megatrends: Ten New Directions Transforming Our Lives*, Naisbitt echoes Toffler and applauds the mass public — "along came the communication revolution and with it an extremely well-educated electorate. Today, with instantaneously shared information, we know as much about what's going on as our representatives and we know it just as quickly." Naisbitt continues his rose-colored vision in the same definite tone: "The fact is we have outlived the historical usefulness of representative democracy and we all sense intuitively that it is obsolete. Furthermore, we have grown more confident of our own ability to make decisions about how institutions, including government and corporations, should operate."[4]

Naisbitt emphasizes how initiatives arising from direct citizen action, with media involvement, will transform our political-governmental system. Toffler goes further to embrace the romantic seductiveness inherent in the possibilities for citizens using different forms of two-way communication to become more participatory in decisions relating to political life. Despite the fact that both viewpoints are based on the false premises of a citizenry equipped with detailed knowledge of public policy matters and a latent desire to participate extensively, the principle of a communication-based method to decide political and governmental issues—what might be called "videocracy"—excites a growing number of people. The American attraction to mechanical gadgets that make any of life's activities easier and more convenient comes into play in this regard.

One representative—and enthusiastic—expression of the potential embodied in the new technology is *Video Democracy* by Richard Hollander. Tellingly subtitled "the vote-from-home revolution," the book argues that the linking of the computer to interactive, cable television systems allows for greater fulfillment of Rousseau's ideal of pure and direct democracy. Although he traces the heritage of mistrust about direct democracy—including discussions of Jefferson's distinction between a republic and a democracy, Tocqueville's fear of a "tyranny of the majority," and James Bryce's related concern about "fatalism of the multitude" in *The American Commonwealth*—Hollander still finds the different instruments of two-way communication considerably appealing, an opportunity to enhance the role citizens play in making governmental decisions.

After describing the decline in political participation in recent years, Hollander states: "Once the two-way cable or related technology is installed, then America has a true opportunity to reverse more than a generation of apathy. Politics can again be what those who dreamed about democracy had in mind. Civic affairs can be a part of everyday existence. Video democracy offers a new lease on life for a system noted more for lethargy than vigor, for staleness than for innovation."[5] Such a statement is more romantic than realistic. How many people want such a responsibility every day? How many would be adequately informed to render regular decisions? Would judgments be based on reasonable merits or on the emotional response to the personality advocating a certain measure? Would such a system discriminate against those without the new technology or the means to acquire it?

Hollander acknowledges that video democracy is "unwise and unworkable" on federal and state-wide levels. Instead he envisions such direct democracy as operating only locally in villages, towns, and small cities. A household's living room — or, more appropriately, individual media center—would become part of a technologically linked town meeting, where local decisions are debated and resolved. With this new form of governance, the emphasis would be ostensibly on issues, with individuals subordinate, and local parties would no longer be involved in the nomination and election of officeholders. Hollander's blueprint for the future rests on the faith that "Americans would rule themselves with justice, compassion and, most of all, common sense."

As entrancing as this democratic dreaming might be, when it collides with our political life *as it is* legitimate concerns multiply instantly. Practically, "video democracy" could only work in relatively small areas (so much for urban America), and there would be the potential consequences of having devout believers in direct democracy wanting to broaden its boundaries. American communications history teaches that television alters in some way whatever its institutional lenses transmit, shaping the subject to fit the needs of the medium. More significantly, American political history teaches that the universe of voters keeps expanding, as pressures and possibilities present themselves. What Toffler, Naisbitt, Hollander, and others see with such visionary clarity would be, in effect, the ultimate temptation of technology to our republican and democratic order as it has evolved since 1787.

O f the sixteen Amendments to the Constitution ratified since the Bill of Rights, seven have either given more direct involvement to the electorate or broadened the voting franchise. Such measures as enabling women to vote and prohibiting poll taxes are matters of justice, righting wrongs. Other amendments — providing the direct popular election of senators and extending the right to vote to anyone 18 years of age or older — make good sense. Widening the democratic circle even more (and remember, too, the involvement of voters in the growing number of initiatives and referenda as well as primaries and caucuses) raises questions about how much direct participation is too much. Where do we draw the line to avoid abandoning the Founders' bedrock principles of representative democracy and dispersed power? What are the legitimate limits at a time when technology makes it possible to consider a videocracy or a "plebiscitary democracy" instead of a representative one?

An irony of American political life is the fact that, while the universe of potential voters has been expanding, actual participation has been declining. Having the franchise does not necessarily translate into involvement. An irony embedded in this irony is that in recent years the decline in voting has been taking place during a period marked by a definite rise in television watching throughout American households. In the presidential election of 1960 between John Kennedy and Richard Nixon, 63.1 percent of the eligible electorate voted—this at a time when TV-viewing averaged a little over five hours per day. By 1988, with the average up to approximately seven hours of viewing a day in a household, the turnout on the presidential level (George Bush vs. Michael Dukakis) was down to 50.16 percent, the lowest rate since 1924. (Except for a small increase in voting in 1984 in the race between Ronald Reagan and Walter Mondale, there has been a decline in each presidential election from 1960 through 1988.)

Admittedly, the motivations for voting or deciding not to vote are complex. Being properly registered is a problem for some people. Seeing a definite reason for taking the effort is another element. The centrism of American politics, with just two principal parties competing for what is perceived to be the most vote-rewarding middle ground, means that people out of the political mainstream find the choices blandly unappealing. The emphasis on television in campaigning is also now being recognized as a factor. In this era of smokeless politics, Bismarck's century-old chestnut—"Politics is like sausage. Neither should be viewed in the making"—carries new meaning for an American voter.

Before the 1960s, the party apparatus used to energize the electorate, helping to get people involved. Now, with much greater reliance on television as the intermediary, there are certain consequences that come from the use of this medium. For many individuals, politics becomes just another spectator sport, one of the many forms of competition transmitted on the tube. What they see taking place is occurring on the stage within the box that provides so much entertainment. Of course, there are periodic messages of information, but they conform to the requirements of the medium, too. People (in some cases, tired or distracted or marginally interested) watch these messages—journalistic reports, paid ads, special campaign programs, whatever—with the same eyes as they view other television fare. Responses are similar—meaning, in great measure, spectatorial. Voting demands making decisions and taking action, two processes certain kinds of spectators might find overly involving and against their videotic inclinations.

It is possible to make too much of the connection between the concurrent decline in voting and the rise in television viewing. The fallout from the Vietnam War, Watergate, and the Iranian hostage ordeal along with the recent emphasis on negativeness and superficial symbolism as opposed to substantive policy debate gives new justification to the old complaint about elected officials. "I never vote," one person allegedly told a reporter earlier this century, "It only encourages them."

Democratic cynicism aside, there are ways of using contemporary (and future) communications technology — especially television — to invigorate American political life. The most difficult task in working out the proper relationship between this technology and our political life involves drawing the appropriate line. Participatory, civic education deserves to be expanded and enhanced. Experiments in direct democracy through two-way communication links should be rejected as temptations without redeeming merits. Back in 1787, when the authors of the Constitution had finished their work in Philadelphia, a woman called out to Benjamin Franklin, "Well, doctor, what have we got — a republic or a monarchy?" Franklin responded: "A republic, if you can keep it." Today's technology offers a new test to keeping the republic.

Two compelling and sensible arguments in defense of education over the "vote-from-home" possibility are F. Christopher Arterton's book *Teledemocracy: Can Technology Protect Democracy?* and *The Electronic Commonwealth: The Impact of New Media Technologies on Democratic Politics* by Arterton, Jeffrey B. Abramson, and Gary R. Orren. Unlike Hollander's idealism of an engaged and involved citizenry in *Video Democracy*, these two other studies of the same territory repeatedly caution against becoming overly optimistic in considering whether new technology will actually improve democratic practices in the years ahead. In *Teledemocracy*, Arterton reaches his conclusions after a systematic analysis of "thirteen different projects in which elites set out to encourage political activity by citizens." Classifying the projects as "plebiscites" or "dialogues," Arterton sees much greater potential in the dialogue projects entailing civic education about governmental policies or processes than in plebiscitarian efforts involving voter reaction of one kind or another.

Illustrations of the effectiveness of teledemocratic projects in education and awareness include "Berks Community Television," which operates in Reading, Pennsylvania, "Alaska's Legislative Teleconferencing Network," and "North Carolina's Open Public Events Network (OPEN/net)" as high-tech undertakings where "policy-making was opened to more citizens than normally participate through traditional institutions." In each case local or state officials learned what citizens thought about issues or legislation. The citizens, in turn, became more knowledgeable about governmental affairs.

By contrast, in evaluating plebiscites made possible by the new technology—such as the "Upper Arlington Town Meeting," conducted by the QUBE cable system in Columbus, Ohio, in 1978, "The Des Moines Health Vote '82," and "Alternatives for Washington," which took place from 1974 through 1976—Arterton discovers limited citizen participation. In other words, technology can make any living room a voting booth, but that does not mean people want to be politically plugged-in, even when local matters are being decided. Assessment of the individual projects leads to the important conclusion that "the available evidence contradicts the assertion by advocates of direct teledemocracy that once citizens realize their actions will really determine outcomes, rates of participation will rise."[6] So much for the romance of Rousseau becoming a reality because of the communications revolution.

The technology for making American political life less of a televised spectator sport exists and should be cultivated to develop more maturely and completely. On a national scale C-SPAN, which began in 1979, is a continuing lesson in civic education, as a citizen has the opportunity to watch governmental and political proceedings as well as take part in telephonic discussions with public figures and journalists. However, the regular viewership of C-SPAN is relatively small (in the neighborhood of a million people, according to the *Electronic Commonwealth*), and there is constant competition from so many other channels. As Arterton correctly points out in *Teledemocracy*, television is primarily—and overwhelmingly—a medium of entertainment. Indeed, he notes that there were more calls to North Carolina's

OPEN/net when the commercial networks were airing advertisements, evidence of random dial-switching rather than sustained involvement. Zapping with a remote control device to avoid ads and deliberating public issues are mutually exclusive activities — or should be. The last sentence of Arterton's book — "Teledemocracy offers us improvements in democracy, not a major transformation nor a final fulfillment"— provides a tempered, reasonable appraisal of the situation.[7]

Idealistic futurologists notwithstanding, the new communications technology does not automatically and directly lead to a new system of electronic voting on matters great and small. (In fact, two-way television experiments, such as QUBE, were flops because most subscribers to the systems lacked the interest and motivation to participate interactively about any subject — sports, fashion trends, television itself.) This technology, though, can be remarkably instructional, yielding more sophisticated political involvement within the existing democratic order for those who take the initiative.

Observers of the emerging diverse forms of communications technology have already identified the phenomenon of "cocooning" and noted the rise in "personal privatization" as social consequences of the popular and widespread usage of these instruments. Increasingly, the ready availability of multi-channel television, advanced audio systems, personal computers, and other machinery of modernity drive Americans home. For many, a residence becomes a plugged-in cocoon, with each family member selecting the desired mode and type of communication. More of life is "mediated" in this environment. There is less direct experience with the world beyond one's door. Public involvement, being out with others for whatever reason, declines as there is greater emphasis on private activities within the house or apartment.

Moreover, there is a growing trend for publishers and editors at newspapers and magazines to deliver reader-tailored publications — in some cases through the fax machine and its progeny as well as through computer networks. People will choose what they want to receive. A subscriber to an electronic newspaper or magazine will have the opportunity to determine the types of articles of greatest personal relevance and attraction. This selection process might — or might not — include news, analysis, and commentary about our political life or international affairs that affect our country. American individualism of high-tech vintage flourishes at the expense of genuine, living and breathing, community.

As the communications revolution continues to offer more and different opportunities for information and diversion, acquiring a civic education of some depth and discrimination will be, paradoxically, both easier and harder. It will be easier because what Ithiel de Sola Pool called the "technologies of freedom" open up so many new possibilities — additional television and radio channels and networks, greater numbers of publications, teletext and videotext data usage, delivery of various kinds of material via fax machines, and so forth. The volume of potentially useful messages grows, with access to them rapid. Conversely, being civically informed will be more difficult because of fragmentation throughout the media. More outlets, many highly specialized, reduce the significance of "mass" as a concept. In fact, communications cognoscenti talk about "the imminent demise of the mass media." In television alone, as one illustration, the percentage of households watching the three major networks during prime time dropped 27 percent from 1970 to 1989, according to Nielsen Media Research.

This greater segmentation and specialization can result in the erosion of a basic, common body of information that constitutes the citizens' knowledge of public affairs. A principal premise behind the Jeffersonian notion of an enlightened citizenry was that people would form judgments and make decisions based on a shared pool of facts and opinions. Now, with the wealth of specialized media sources, the sharing is more difficult as individuals satisfy their interests and needs through the free choice of what technology offers. The marketplace of ideas is becoming so crowded that having the chance to think about public matters is more of a challenge for the citizenry.

The political implications of such phenomena as "cocooning" and "personal privatization" are profound. Statecraft and stagecraft become even more intertwined. Public figures realize that to deliver a message they have to attract the attention of people in communications, who will decide whether and how to treat the message. With television the dominant medium for making this second-hand connection with the greatest number of citizens, the personality of the public figure is a critical concern. Should someone's personality — at least what is transmitted for us to see and hear — *not* be congenial to the requirements of television, it will be difficult to get a message across. In the realm of campaigning for office, it is possible, of course, for an adroit media consultant to produce commercials that avoid focusing on the personality. News coverage, however, is vastly different. While running and governing, how the public figure projects himself or herself, in spoken word and through action, is influential both to journalistic decision making (what makes it on the air) and to citizen appraisal (how people react and what they think).

If coverage of politics and government became just one subject among many available to a person, how many would elect to take this material? Achieving some kind of consensus would become increasingly difficult because people's exposure to information about public affairs would vary so widely. Some citizens, tuned into CNN and C-SPAN and receiving a wealth of printed dispatches about politics and government, might be models of civic awareness. Others, absorbed by ESPN or MTV and drowning in sports statistics or news about pop culture fads, would have but passing acquaintance with civic life and world affairs.

Information about public affairs is a marginal concern for the majority of Americans. Former NBC political correspondent Ken Bode, now director of DePauw University's Center for Contemporary Media, illustrates this with a story about the night of the New Hampshire primary in 1988. Writing in *TV Guide* he reports that anchor Tom Brokaw called him over that evening — "'Bode,' he growled, 'this campaign coverage is costing us in the ratings. The viewers don't like politics. It goes on too long. They're tired of it.'" As Bode observes, "This was the first of the nation's primaries. There were still a dozen candidates in the race. The nomination was up for grabs in both parties. Viewers already bored? Costing us in the news ratings?" Television values and democratic values keep colliding, with the prospect of creating even more questions for the future.

As the new technological possibilities reconstitute the mass into smaller, like-minded segments, people in communications are scrambling to target their messages in the most appropriate and effective ways. In many cases commercial concerns — from institutional survival to increased profits — help dictate the decisions.

The concern is to discover what will work to attract and keep potential readers, viewers, and listeners. Due to this fragmentation and competition, the content of messages is in a constant state of redefinition. With this happening, what will be the fate of our traditional modes of learning about matters of public significance? To what extent will the temptation of specialization determine the substance of communications? At what cost and consequences?

The implications for the conduct of statecraft within this technologically rich media environment are enormous. Gone are the days when public figures could count on the citizenry being collectively and continually exposed to political and governmental information, the daily drop-by-drop dose of civic news. The sheer number and variety of messages vying for one's attention means that effective stagecraft will become more important to gaining an electoral following and to governing with popular support. The ascent of television, which produced the Age of Personality, brought the relationship between statecraft and stagecraft to a new proximity. The future promises even greater intimacy between statecraft and stagecraft, as those in political life discover ways of visiting so many private cocoons to penetrate America's public mind.

Postscript: The Theater of War, The War as Theater, and Other Matters

"Did You Watch the War Last Night?"

The large newspaper headline asked a startling, yet, given the circumstances, predictable question. The realms of government and communications intertwined during the Persian Gulf War in 1991 to produce what was repeatedly called "a real war in real time"— a genuine "living room war." Because of the new, sophisticated media technology, the most serious policy action a government can take—deciding that human life is worth risking to achieve certain objectives — turned into a continuing drama played out on television screens across America and around the world.

In this Age of Personality, stars were born quickly — General Norman Schwarzkopf, Pentagon briefer Lieutenant General Thomas Kelly, CNN's Peter Arnett, NBC's Arthur Kent, dubbed "the Scud Stud." The Cable News Network transformed itself into the Cable War News Network. And people at home became the ultimate spectators, interrupting work, or social life, or sleep to tune in the war. There was an unreal, almost surreal quality to the reality. Missiles exploded in front of our eyes, and we munched popcorn on the sofa.

The Persian Gulf War provides valuable lessons about statecraft and stagecraft for today and tomorrow. Before, during, and after the war, the media were much more than messengers of news about the conflict. They were players — actors, if you will — of considerable consequence. In fact, as the war itself unfolded, other battles raged. Journalists fought with military officials in the Gulf and in Washington to secure more details and greater

103

access to information, and news people skirmished among themselves scrambling for stories.

The intensity of the coverage and its immediacy were distinc-
tive factors marking the involvement of the media in what happened during the Gulf crisis. From Iraq's invasion of Kuwait on
August 2, 1990, until the war began on January 16, 1991, much
of the communication between Iraq and the American-led coalition took place as a result of television or radio broadcasts. Iraqi
leader Saddam Hussein would give a speech on his country's TV
or appear at a staged event with, say, hostages, and his views or
acts were immediately amplified. For his part, President George
Bush was not shy about speaking his mind in front of cameras
and microphones for the widest possible distribution here and
abroad. Many of his statements were personally directed at Saddam Hussein — on one occasion the president vowed: "He's going
to get his ass kicked"— and these remarks in particular received
repeated play because they conformed to both the personality
orientation and conflict appeal of the media. A slashing sound-
bite, with war looming, might not be helpful on the diplomatic
front, but it sure gets attention on the homefront and shows rhetorical resolve as well as symbolic spine internationally.

The massive military build-up was rivaled only by the dis-
patching of reporters and other communications personnel to
chronicle whatever might take place. As the United Nations–
mandated deadline of January 15th for Iraq to leave Kuwait ap-
proached, some media sources even seemed to catch war fever.
For example, the "CBS Evening News" bannered its coverage of
the Gulf crisis as "Countdown to Confrontation," ceremoniously
ticking off the days for over a week until January 15th. CNN carried reports under the heading "Deadline in the Desert." Although
journalistically justifiable — a firm date did exist — the approach
conveyed to the public the expectation of immediate action. To
delay a military operation much beyond the deadline could create a perception of weakness, something the president and other
leaders certainly wanted to avoid. The point, of course, is that
the media in their way and with their techniques of emphasis
contributed to the pressure for beginning the hostilities.

And war came January 16th — just as the evening network news
programs on ABC, CBS, and NBC began their broadcasts in the
Eastern and Midwestern time zones. For the next several days,

the work of a high-tech military and a high-tech communications industry kept Americans and other people both fascinated and fearful. The live reports, whether from Baghdad, Riyadh, or Tel Aviv, were especially compelling. What we were collectively witnessing was neither a movie nor a mini-series, but a flesh-and-blood war with danger and death within camera or sound range.

At the beginning of the blanket coverage, the novelty of watching a U.S. Patriot missile intercept an Iraqi Scud kept viewers engrossed. In addition, seeing journalists give reports while wearing gas masks or seeking cover from an attack provided a more compelling meaning to the metaphor of a "global village." However, about a week after the war started, the novelty and emotional euphoria subsided as serious questions about the media and their involvement in what was happening in the Gulf began to circulate in the government and throughout the public. As this occurred, news people covering the war launched their own offensive against the military-imposed rules for collecting and transmitting information, and journalists defended CNN's decision to continue providing reports from Iraq. That CNN is received in over a hundred countries was an aspect of the debate that did not receive appropriate attention. An international news organization of this type has different, in some cases greater, responsibilities to produce fair and factual reporting because its work is immediately available to a worldwide audience.

The very size of media representation became an issue. According to *The Media At War: The Press and the Persian Gulf Conflict*, a June 1991 report of the Gannett Foundation, "more than 1,400 correspondents" were assigned to war coverage.[1] Such journalistic deployment suggests a commitment to rooting out any piece of news with even tangential relevance. "The news watch never stops," some all-news radio stations boast. For over six weeks — the cease-fire was announced February 28th — the war became what the news watched.

Besides the sheer volume of information, the velocity and style of its transmission turned into a double-edged sword. Americans learned about many events as they were occurring — but so, through the efficiency of modern communications, did Iraqis. The world of both friends and foes has simultaneous access to a media report, especially from a source like CNN. George Bush

and other high-level members of the administration often commented on what was taking place by referring to TV coverage.
They were watching, too. Given these new circumstances, what
information does a government engaged in war divulge, and
when is the most appropriate time to release such information?
Do you wait, for example, to announce a large bombing mission
until the last aircraft is either back or accounted for? What about
reporters who see bombers take off? Should they report what is
happening at the moment or delay such news until the military
makes a statement? Do you show videotape of prisoners of war
and air their statements?

Questions of this nature now abound, and the wisdom of Solo-
mon would be taxed doing justice to them. In America, with our
heritage of a free press and the First Amendment, censorship is
not only a dirty word but a fighting word. The guidelines established by the U.S. Defense Department sought to maintain as
much control over war-related information as possible. Access
to people and places was restricted; military officials reviewed
reports from the field, removing sensitive information or changing the wording used, and briefings emphasized exactly what the
American and coalition commanders wanted the public to know.
This part of the communications environment had changed markedly since the Vietnam War, and that fact along with the desire
to avoid anything resembling the Vietnam experience shaped the
military's thinking about how to deal with the media during the
Persian Gulf War.

Journalists, however, became frustrated while attempting to
offer complete and accurate coverage of the conflict. Such frus-
tration is nothing new, but the public kept seeing it because so
much attention was being devoted to any information about the
war. Television reports caught journalists in the act of gathering
material. Viewers could see that the edited or produced result
of reporting was more tidy and professional than the day-to-day
collection process. Over and over, news people seemed to be bad-
gering or doubting military speakers. Henry Allen of the *Washington Post* described the widely shared American perception of
the correspondents a month into the war: "The Persian Gulf press
briefings are making reporters look like fools, nit-pickers and
egomaniacs; like dilettantes who have spent exactly none of their
lives on the end of a gun or even a shovel; dinner party com-

mandos, slouching inquisitors, collegiate spitball artists; people who have never been in a fistfight much less combat; a whining, self-righteous, upper-middle-class mob jostling for whatever tiny flakes of fame may settle on their shoulders like some sort of Pulitzer Prize dandruff."

Some Americans went so far as to question the loyalty and patriotism of the journalists. Peter Arnett of CNN became the target of attacks from Senator Alan Simpson and others for remaining in Baghdad to report what was taking place there. That Arnett's work was subject to Iraqi censorship was highly objectionable to many people. Whose side are the media on? became a frequently asked question. We're just trying to do our job — which is different from the the military's or government's — was the common response.

The debate about the involvement of the media in a crisis like the Persian Gulf War will continue. The volume and velocity of communications messages today create a force that can be counter to the policy objectives of the government and the military. For journalists, balancing their professional responsibilities and their obligations as citizens becomes more difficult. For those in public life, conducting the people's business with some fidelity to democratic accountability now demands closer attention to what the media are doing.

Besides the velocity and volume, the type of message — especially the way it is presented — is significant. The most compelling and memorable coverage of the Persian Gulf War came to us via television images, either live reports involving action or dramatic taped footage. To be sure the military made effective use of what are called "good visuals" in numerous briefings by showing tapes of the air campaign and "smart bombs" in action. Implicit in these demonstrations — the public did not see many misses — was the message that the new, expensive, high-tech hardware works. The Pentagon had not just been buying $800 hammers with tax money in recent years.

During the Gulf War, the military maintained what control they could over the images television projected and the public witnessed. There was much grumbling in the media of the "sanitized" nature of the coverage. Human casualties and suffering were kept at a distance, out of camera range, if at all possible. A paradox of the reporting is that the wall-to-wall coverage was criticized for being so imcomplete and unrevealing. Quality can never be confused with quantity.

Following the cease-fire, President Bush exclaimed: "By God, we've kicked the Vietnam syndrome once and for all." However, the afterglow of the U.S.-led victory began to dim when the public started to see disturbing images of the war's aftermath. In the most striking example, the plight of the Kurdish people living in Iraq but opposed to Saddam Hussein received extended treatment. Iraqi forces battled with the Kurds, driving thousands to squalid refugee camps. The images of children and older people struggling to survive served as a counterpoint to the earlier wartime images of military success. Winning the war was not supposed to lead to a situation like this, Americans thought.

Coverage of the condition of the Kurds turned into a case study in media attention leading directly to governmental policy. The coverage, especially the television images and still pictures — the April 15th cover of *Newsweek* was a close-up picture of the bloody face of a little girl; in large print the question, "Why Won't He Help Us?" was directed at Bush — helped force the United States to get involved in supplying food and medical aid. There was a definite progression to the policy action: (1) The image-dominated coverage aroused emotions. (2) Those emotions stimulated concern and thinking. (3) That concern and thinking coalesced quickly into a public attitude or opinion that something should be done. (4) Pressure then developed to take direct action — with formal governmental measures the result. Without the media attention, chances are that the United States would have treated what was happening to the Kurds as a domestic dispute within Iraq — something beyond the principal objective of liberating Kuwait and, hence, *not* politically justifiable.

Although there was substantial criticism of the Bush Administration for stopping the fighting prematurely — Saddam Hussein was still very much in power and ruthlessly eager to crush internal opposition — George Bush himself came out of the war with considerable and continuing public approval. One survey shortly after the cease-fire measured Bush's popularity at an astonishing 91 percent, and polls in subsequent months hovered in the 70 percent range.

During the Gulf crisis, Bush ultimately came into sharper focus for Americans and for the world at large. Until Iraq's invasion of Kuwait, the president had been chided for (among other things) excessive caution in responding to events and for an overreliance on private, one-to-one communications to transact affairs of state. As events in the Mideast unfolded, however, these traits began to be interpreted differently. Execution of the government's foreign policy necessitated a deliberate, methodical strategy — political, diplomatic, and military — as well as the sustained participation of a unified coalition working in concert with the United Nations. To orchestrate this multinational cooperation required direct, usually telephonic, personal communication and persuasion.

As Americans watched the plans being implemented, many looked at the president's approach to governing from a new perspective. Bush's method of leadership worked in achieving its principal objective — and the nation saluted a victorious commander-in-chief. That salute, though, took time in coming.

During the months before the war, it was difficult to interpret and judge what Bush was actually doing or even intending to do. In mid-November, three-and-a-half months into the crisis, Senator Richard Lugar said: "I think the president must lay out now to the nation and the Congress specifically what our aims are." That the Indiana Republican publicly urged Bush to articulate America's "aims" at that late date suggests a failure by the president of making a coherent case for the policy he was pursuing. Emphasizing behind-the-scenes statecraft came at the expense of effective stagecraft. The telephone rather than television was Bush's favored instrument of communication, and the lack of a balanced approach to private *and* public message delivery left people (including a respected senator) wanting a more definite and cogent rationale.

The problem in communicating to the citizenry in a deliberate and meaningful way was nothing new for the president. In fact, an argument can be made that the much-despised "wimp" label stuck as long as it did because Bush failed to project a distinct image with specific qualities for several years. In the absence of an explicit effort of self-dramatization with a political purpose behind it, the media are more likely to engage in labeling of their own. Bush's inattention to the skills of public presentation and persuasion is long standing and a principal reason why political commentators frequently point out that the president's support is "shallow." A strong, emotional connection between a leader and the citizens does not exist.

During the late summer and fall of 1990, Bush's difficulties with stagecraft and image-making persisted. At the beginning of the troop deployment in the Gulf, there were jarring scenes of the president on vacation in Maine racing through a round of golf or out fishing, while military personnel sacrificed vacations and family time to go to the desert. Bush did not seem to be having a particularly good time, and the symbolism was wrong. The public wondered if there was, indeed, a crisis, and, if so, whether the president was being somewhat insensitive.

Interestingly, almost exactly a year later, when Mikhail Gorbachev was temporarily removed from power as president of the Soviet Union by hard-line Communists and the military in an attempted yet unsuccesful coup, Bush immediately returned to Washington from his vacation in Maine. He did not remain in the White House throughout the crisis, but a lesson had been learned. The administration, too, sought to make effective use of the new web of sophisticated communications technology linking all parts of the world. According to a report in the *Washington Post*, "One administration policymaker said that his first consideration on hearing about the coup was not how to cable instructions on the U.S. reaction to American diplomats, but how to get a statement on CNN that would shape the response of all the allies. 'Diplomatic communications just can't keep up with CNN,' he said." International relations have been transformed by the communications revolution, and many analysts rightly see the media as engines of change and critical participants in unfolding developments.

In the battle over the federal budget during the fall of 1990, Bush once again had serious problems communicating with the coherence and inspiration required today. Abandoning the pledge of his 1988 election slogan—"Read my lips: No new taxes"—the president made matters worse by not looking to be in command as budget proposals circulated through the White House and Congress. At one point in the debate, when a reporter asked Bush a question about taxes, the president (who was out jogging) pointed to his buttocks and invited the journalist, "Read my hips." The media made much of that moment, and the country became even more confused because Bush did not seem to take either his former slogan or the current problem seriously. Later, an Oval Office, prime-time speech to produce support for a budget compromise measure backfired, as Republicans in the House of Representatives voted against the president. An editorial in the *New York Times*, titled "The Empty Pulpit," concluded: "The deficit is a cancer. The public needs to be rallied to support an effective remedy. What does the President do about that? He dithers."

Bush's success in building an international coalition against Iraq and in preparing for possible war demonstrated leadership ability in stark contrast to what he did with the budget and other domestic problems. Highlighting the differences, *Time* (in its January 7, 1991 issue) named "The Two George Bushes" the magazine's "Men of the Year." The phrases "In the Gulf: Bold Vision" and "At Home: No Vision" led off two detailed articles, one flattering, the other critical. More and more people were seeing the complexity of George Bush and also the lack of a comprehensive and balanced style of presidential leadership.

Despite the doubts of Senator Lugar and others about whether Bush had made a compelling case for military action, once the Gulf War started the president became much more sensitive to the symbolic significance of images. Shots of him praying at the chapel at Camp David, or taking a solitary walk around the White House grounds, or working in the Oval Office on the precise wording of his final "ultimatum" to Iraq were not only reassuring but important to the public's perception of a deliberative commander-in-chief. In addition, his speeches and press conference performances seemed more meaningful and measured — appropriate to the time and situation. Like the campaign of 1988, Bush paid close attention to effective stagecraft at a critical period when such attention was necessary.

One wonders what to expect of a Bush campaign for re-election in 1992. At this writing the president and his advisors are planning the race. Will stagecraft be a significant concern? More importantly, will the incumbent president attempt to bring campaigning and governing closer together? Writing about 1988 in *Pledging Allegiance: The Last Campaign of the Cold War*, Sidney Blumenthal observes:

If Dukakis attempted to divide emotion from action, Bush
tried to split politics from policy. Politics had to be conducted
in the arena, where the candidate was at the mercy of a public
drama. It was ruled by the law of the jungle, the survival of
the fittest. Policy, however, was guided by "the best people,"
as he once called them. It was crafted within the bureaucra-
cies of Washington in which Bush had risen over the decades.
Precisely because Bush was so obviously one of "the best people," he had had to prove himself by claw and fang. The Dar-
winian struggle was the price he paid for the opportunity to
be himself.

"The American people are wonderful when it comes to understanding when a campaign ends and the work of business
begins," said President-elect Bush in his first postelection news
conference. The week of his inauguration, Bush was interviewed on ABC "News" by Barbara Walters, who asked him
about the campaign by which he had won the White House.
"That's history," he said. "That doesn't mean anything any-
more." The campaign had been an unpleasant necessity, but
was otherwise of no consequence. It had illumined no truths
about the country of the candidates that had meaning beyond
election day. "That's history" was among Bush's favorite phrases.
He used it whenever he did not want to be held accountable
for what he had done before, even if it had happened yesterday. The past is weightless; history is bunk.[2]

Entering the 1992 race, Bush brings with him over three years
of a presidency marked by international upheaval and serious
economic problems affecting the government itself and the country as a whole. For him, recent history will be anything but bunk,
and questions about the future—especially how to resolve festering problems within America—will demand answers of one kind
or another. Balance between politics and policy, between foreign
and domestic affairs, and—yes—between statecraft and stagecraft will be crucial to electoral success.

If the mid-term election of 1990 offered any clues about the
future of American political life, politicians and the public at
large can anticipate a continuing preoccupation with the negative messages that disgust so many citizens. Across the country
during the fall of 1990, living rooms at times resembled battle-

fields as candidates engaged in spot-to-spot combat of attack and counterattack advertising. The nasty, bare-knuckled commercials appeared in races large and small, and were as favored by Democrats as Republicans. What passed for political discourse in these campaigns seemed more inspired by the possibility of destroying an opponent than actually of dealing with issues in a constructive or informative manner.

So much mud emanated from American television sets that journalists in print and on TV took to analyzing ads for distortions and falsehoods as regular political features. In addition, calls for a general clean-up of the campaign environment grew louder, as more and more people became fed up. Behind the efforts to monitor the spots and to work to foster a better political climate is the realization that electoral fraud now occurs more often in full public view before a single ballot is cast. It used to be different. However, stricter election laws (with closer attention to precise vote counting) as well as the decline of party organizations (with what was formerly their machinelike process of gathering votes) make it much more difficult to steal an election at the polls. Today, though, "deceit, trickery, intentional dishonesty" (a dictionary definition of fraud) commonly take place on TV screens, as candidates compete for attention and support.

Negative commercials are not created equally. Some are produced to be — in the preferred term of political consultants — "comparative." In these ads factual information about the record or character of the opposing candidate emphasizes the worst. And as long as a spot is truthful and accurate, it is difficult to find much fault with such a message. However, electoral fraud of this new variety does occur when a commercial about a political rival is conceived and executed without regard for any standards of honesty or even accuracy. Bending the truth with an eerie image or an emotionally charged phrase can ultimately break a candidate.

What we see happening in political communication today is, in part, a consequence of the 1988 presidential campaign. Negative advertising took center stage then and has remained there. In a report released in 1990 after two years of study, the Markle Commission on the Media and the Electorate found that "the Bush campaign was the single most important source of influence on voters, largely through the use of advertising. Very little paid political advertising by either camp, however, dealt with issues that concerned voters such as the budget deficit, drugs or health care."[3] The commercials that had the most impact were those that attacked Bush's opponent, Michael Dukakis. The Markle report classified certain Bush spots as "misleading": the portrayals of the Massachusetts prison furlough program, the pollution in Boston harbor, and Dukakis's veto of a bill about saying the Pledge of Allegiance in schools.

Although slow in responding and in "going negative," the Dukakis campaign ended up with dirty hands of its own. A survey conducted at the Political Commercial Archive of the University of Oklahoma found that forty-nine of the ninety-seven Dukakis TV ads could be classified as negative or comparative, while fifteen of the forty ads for Bush were negative or comparative. More compelling productions, along with earlier and repeated airings, proved to be more important than the actual quantity of spots broadcast.

A prime lesson of the 1988 campaign is that an opponent's charge demands a swift, equally sharp countercharge. In this circumstance, of course, two negatives do *not* equal a positive. They just accelerate the cycle of attack messages and contribute to a political atmosphere of negativism and public cynicism. Now, in the aftermath of 1988, candidates across the country have repeatedly made negative commercials focal points of their campaigns. Office-seekers and their consultants think: "The approach was successful for George Bush, and he didn't suffer lingering public disapproval. Why not follow the leader?" The modern, sophisticated communications technology plays a role, too. Ads responding to an attack can be produced and on the air in a matter of six hours or so, propelling the cycle at a previously unknown — and alarming — speed.

Despite the greater emphasis on a tactic of televised attacks, a backlash movement is taking shape. At the heart of this uncoordinated undertaking is the understanding that a hit-and-run or drive-by-shooting approach to political communication can, indeed, encourage fraud and deception and character assassination.

On the governmental level, Congress is debating several proposals to reduce the amount of money spent on television commercials, to expand the possibilities for longer (maybe even free) broadcast messages, and to demand that candidates take much greater personal responsibility for what is shown and said about themselves and their opponents. Many negative commercials are explicit attacks on rivals — without seeing or hearing the sponsoring candidate. The proposed legislation would ensure more direct accountability by having the candidate endorse his or her message in full public view.

For political consultants, the growing controversy over political negativism has led to some institutional soul-searching. There is discussion among members of the American Association of Political Consultants to create a self-regulating enforcement mechanism with the authority to censure political hirelings responsible for producing deceptive spots. A board of consultants would determine what's fair and what's not. Even Lee Atwater, architect of Bush's 1988 campaign, came to see the danger and ethical dubiousness of negative, attack-oriented politics. Shortly before his death from cancer March 29, 1991, Atwater apologized to many former opponents, and he wrote: "I used to say that the president might be kinder and gentler, but I wasn't going to be. How wrong I was. There is nothing more important in life than human beings."

In journalism the realization of the impact of negative spots on individual campaigns and on the whole political climate is resulting in more sustained scrutiny of the ads as they appear. Determining what might be fraudulent or deceptive is not an exact science and frequently is in the eye of the beholder. But journalists in print and broadcasting are professionally situated to analyze commercials for factual and contextual accuracy. Probing examination and exposure of misleading elements can provide a valuable outside check on a unique type of advertising. As it currently stands, political spots are subject to no regulation, and communication law exempts such appeals from censorship by broadcasters. Critical yet fair continuing coverage to identify distortions has a place in journalism. An irony, though, is that with increasing frequency candidates are using these same journalistic appraisals to slam their opponents for deception. Such counterattacks serve their purpose of repeated exposure, but they unfortunately contribute to the downward spiral of campaigning. Negative ads feed off of earlier negative ads, accentuating the negative throughout.

Back in 1955, when television was just beginning to become

the new stage of American politics, Walter Lippmann warned in *The Public Philosophy:* "If there is a dividing line between liberty and license, it is where freedom of speech is no longer respected as a procedure of the truth and becomes the unrestricted right to exploit the ignorance, and to incite the passions, of the people. Then freedom is such a hullabaloo of sophistry, propaganda, special pleading, lobbying, and salesmanship that it is difficult to remember why freedom of speech is worth the pain and trouble of defending it."[4] The current concern over negative advertising signals a desire to deal with a form of license that not only exploits ignorance and incites passions but also promotes electoral fraud. If political commercials on television are the window through which we see much of our democratic life, especially our candidates running for office, the view we receive should be as clear as possible. Cleaning the window will require the collective work of government officials, people in the media, political consultants, and the citizens themselves.

One proposal to consider would allow a candidate a full minute of air-time at the cost of a thirty-second spot, provided the candidate appears personally to make his or her pitch. Such an arrangement gives the candidate more time to deliver a message, with the politician taking complete responsibility for what is said. The longer format runs counter to the pattern of half-minute (or shorter) appeals, enhancing the distinctiveness of the ad in the mind of the public. The candidate would be free to talk about his or her opponent, but the dirt would be on the speaker's hands — or lips. It is difficult to imagine an entire sixty seconds of personal attack. Should it happen, voters would be inclined to see the candidate as a negative, nay-saying individual without specific governmental objectives. Doubling the time while continuing to pay the cost of a thirty-second spot adds substance to political discourse and might encourage even greater development of discussions about solving problems. Broadcasting associations, networks, and individual stations could perform a genuine civic duty by supporting and implementing such a plan.

A much more ambitious proposal is outlined by Paul Taylor in his book *See How They Run: Electing the President in an Age of Mediaocracy.* Taylor writes: "Starting with the 1992 campaign, each major candidate for President should be given five minutes of free time a night — on alternating nights — *simultaneously* on every television and radio station in the country for the final five weeks of the campaign." Under the plan, the presidential candidate or the vice-presidential running mate would talk directly into the cameras and microphones for each of the five-minute appearances: "No Willie Horton. No opponent. No surrogate. No journalists."[5] Taylor's proposal has considerable merit, but the exclusive focus on the presidency leaves out all the other elective offices and their growing attraction to and use of negative advertising. One would hope, however, that candidates in general would take their cues from the presidential race and devote more attention to fuller, policy-oriented messages.

Another definite plan to encourage greater emphasis on substance during the presidential election season is outlined in *Nine Sundays: A Proposal for Better Presidential Campaign Coverage*. Developed at Harvard University's Joan Shorenstein Barone Center on the Press, Politics and Public Policy, this methodical and well-reasoned scheme makes the Sunday evenings between Labor Day and Election Day regular occasions when citizens can watch and listen to the candidates for president and vice-president over sustained periods of time. Included during the nine Sundays would be two presidential debates; one debate for the vice-presidential nominees; five detailed discussions with the presidential candidates about issues related to national security, the economy, and social or cultural concerns, and one evening at the end for final speeches by the two presidential hopefuls. The debates and final speeches would be broadcast by ABC, CBS, NBC, and CNN, while the conversations would be aired on a rotating basis by the three largest networks as well as CNN. A prime virtue of this proposal is the regularity of scheduling extended presentations about public affairs as the people focus more attention on the general election. The plan, too, takes into account current economic conditions of commercial television.

There is no shortage of well-meaning, worthwhile suggestions for reform of political communication. Giving these reforms a chance to drive out the negativism and fraud is vastly superior to other remedies for dealing with the cynicism, disillusionment, and apathy of today. During the 1990 mid-term campaign season, called "the election of our discontent" by a number of journalists, several citizen movements across the country worked hard for limitations of office holders' terms, for introducing a "none-of-the-above" option to the ballot, and for making initiatives (instead of public officials) more central to the conduct of government on the state level. These measures resonate and find favor because segments of a disenchanted citizenry think the only way to improve political life is by keeping politicians on a shorter leash. As sincere as such efforts are, they introduce profound structural change when it is really the existing political-media environment that needs attention. Taking some of the pollution out of the political air would do a lot to return citizens to a sunnier disposition toward our democratic enterprise.

In *The Making of the President 1960,* Theodore H. White wrote the first book-length narrative about a presidential election in America. On the first page of Chapter One, he says:

> On election day America is Republican until five or six in the evening. It is in the last few hours of the day that working people and their families vote, on their way home from work or after supper; it is then, at evening, that America goes Democratic if it goes Democratic at all. All of this is invisible, for it is the essence of the act that as it happens it is a mystery in which millions of people each fit one fragment of a total secret together, none of them knowing the shape of the whole.
>
> What results from the fitting together of these secrets is, of course, the most awesome transfer of power in the world — the power to marshal and mobilize, the power to send men to kill or be killed, the power to tax and destroy, the power to create and the responsibility to do so, the power to guide and the responsibility to heal — all committed into the hands of one man. Heroes and philosophers, brave men and vile, have since Rome and Athens tried to make this particular manner of transfer of power work effectively; no people has succeeded at it better, or over a longer period of time, than the Americans. Yet as the transfer of this power takes place, there is nothing to be seen except an occasional line outside a church or school, or a file of people fidgeting in the rain, waiting to enter the booths. No bands play on election day, no troops march, no guns are readied, no conspirators gather in secret headquarters. The noise and the blare, the bands and the screaming, the pageantry and oratory of the long fall campaign, fade on election day. All the planning is over, all effort spent. Now the candidates must wait.[6]

White's prose soars a little higher than it probably should, but the words reflect a seriousness of purpose about the meaning of a presidential campaign. There is something noble to the process and to the exercise of power that is the consequence of an American election.

By contrast, Roger Simon — one of White's many followers in chronicling a presidential campaign — begins *Road Show* by capturing the mood that existed after what happened in 1988. In the preface, Simon says:

> Alone in his bedroom on a dark and stormy night, the presidential candidate was putting the finishing touches on his announcement speech when the devil appeared before him.
>
> "Worry not," the devil said. "I can grant you a victory in the Iowa caucuses. I can give you the New Hampshire primary, the South, New York, California and all the rest. I will even guarantee you the nomination of your party. But in return, you must sell me your soul.
>
> "You must betray all decent principles. You much pander, trivialize and deceive. You must gain victory by exploiting bigotry, fear, envy and greed. And you must conduct a campaign based on lies, sham, hype and distortion."
>
> "So?" the presidential candidate replied. "What's the catch?"[7]

Times change, a master of the obvious might say. However, the changes that have occurred politically since 1960 lead people to think of pacts with the devil rather than of seances with the Founding Fathers. That voter turnout has not matched the 1960 level of 63.1 percent in any presidential year since is as much an indication of citizen distaste as of apathy. Somehow or other, there needs to be a coming back together of the two partners of statecraft: campaigning and governing.

In *Why Americans Hate Politics*, E. J. Dionne, Jr., notes that ideological polarization separating Democrats and Republicans currently results in "a politics of false choices." Voters feel trapped in a crossfire of mass-mediated slogans and sound-bites over such subjects as gender equality and the family or social compassion and personal self-reliance. Politicians seek support without making core concerns the foundations of their campaigns. Once in office, those elected act without giving much thought to the words and ideas that got them there. Reading lips — or hips — can be confusing and depressing. Dionne describes the dead end just down the road when he writes: "Our current political dialogue fails us and leads us to hate politics because it insists on stifling yes/no, either/or approaches that ignore the elements that must come together to create a successful and democratic civic culture. Democracy is built on constant struggle among competing goods, not on an absolute certainty about which goods are paramount. This must be the central theme of a new political center."[8]

Moving beyond "yes/no, either/or" alternatives to a more coherent and purposeful "both/and" centrist consensus will require change in political thinking and communication, will and action. At the moment, stark, combative messages, especially of the nasty or negative variety, cut through the competing media attempts for our attention. The less polarizing statements do not conform to the existing communications climate, and they either fail to reach or to move the public. Here stagecraft enters, from both the left and the right, to join with statecraft.

The need for a different political-media environment is apparent to anyone who has passed a basic civics course. Without changes in the way we learn about and assess public figures and affairs, American political life will continue to be polarized — and frustrating to those who recognize that serious problems demand collective solution. With such changes, more citizens will rediscover direct, vital connections between themselves and the public activities putatively done in their name and certainly paid for with their tax money. In that better time, statecraft and stagecraft will work together in a more harmonious and productive relationship that links public figures and the people in a common endeavor to confront the future.

Notes

Chapter 1
1. Nelson W. Polsby, *Consequences of Party Reform* (New York and Oxford: Oxford University Press, 1983), p. 67.

Chapter 2
1. William Safire, *Safire's Political Dictionary: An Enlarged, Up-to-Date Edition of The New Language of Politics* (New York: Random House, 1978), pp. 323–324.

2. Joe McGinniss, *The Selling of the President 1968* (New York: Trident Press, 1969), pp. 193–194.

3. Ibid., p. 195.

4. Michael Novak, *Choosing Our King: Powerful Symbols in Presidential Politics* (New York: Macmillan, 1974), p. 251.

Chapter 3
1. Jeffrey K. Tulis, *The Rhetorical Presidency* (Princeton, N.J.: Princeton University Press, 1987).

2. Martin Schram, *The Great American Video Game: Presidential Politics in the Television Age* (New York: William Morrow, 1987), p. 26.

3. David S. Broder, *Behind the Front Page: A Candid Look at How News is Made* (New York: Simon and Schuster, 1987), pp. 181–182.

4. George Reedy, *The Twilight of the Presidency*, rev. ed. (New York: New American Library, 1987), p. 112.

5. Ronald Reagan, *Speaking My Mind: Selected Speeches* (New York: Simon and Schuster, 1989), pp. 256–257.

6. Garry Wills, *Reagan's America: Innocents at Home* (Garden City, N.Y.: Doubleday, 1987), p. 123.

7. Richard E. Neustadt, *Presidential Power: The Politics of Leadership from FDR to Carter* (New York: Wiley, 1980), pp. 9–10.

8. Peggy Noonan, *What I Saw at the Revolution: A Political Life in the Reagan Era* (New York: Random House, 1990), p. 268.

9. James Fallows, "The Passionless Presidency," *Atlantic*, May 1979, p. 43.

10. Text of Address to the Nation, July 15, 1979, in *Public Papers of the Presidents of the United States: Jimmy Carter, 1979*, II (Washington, D.C.: U.S. Government Printing Office, 1980), pp. 1236–1237.

11. Richard Nixon, *Leaders* (New York: Warner Books, 1982), p. 342.

Chapter 4

1. Walter Lippmann, *The Phantom Public* (New York: Harcourt, Brace, 1925), pp. 20–21.

2. Ibid., p. 77.

3. W. Russell Neuman, *The Paradox of Mass Politics: Knowledge and Opinion in the American Electorate* (Cambridge, Mass.: Harvard University Press, 1986).

4. Ibid., p. 8 and p. 29.

5. Walter Dean Burnham, *The Current Crisis in American Politics* (New York and Oxford: Oxford University Press, 1982), p. 31.

6. Kathleen Hall Jamieson, *Eloquence in an Electronic Age: The Transformation of Political Speechmaking* (New York and Oxford: Oxford University Press, 1988), p. 10.

7. Kiku Adatto, "TV Tidbits Starve Democracy," *New York Times*, 10 Dec. 1989, Sec. 4, p. 23.

8. Tulis, *Rhetorical Presidency*, p. 80.

9. Lloyd N. Cutler, "Foreign Policy on Deadline," *Foreign Policy*, No. 56 (1984), p. 114.

10. Ibid., p. 118.

Chapter 5

1. Thomas Jefferson, *The Writings of Thomas Jefferson*, ed. Andrew A. Lipscomb and Albert Ellery Bergh (Washington,

D.C.: The Thomas Jefferson Memorial Association, 1905), III, 380–381.

2. Ibid., XI, 224.

3. Michael J. Robinson, "The Media in 1980: Was the Message the Message?" in *The American Elections of 1980*, ed. Austin Ranney (Washington, D.C.: American Enterprise Institute, 1981), pp. 177–178.

4. James David Barber, *The Pulse of Politics: Electing Presidents in the Media Age* (New York: W. W. Norton, 1980), p. 9.

5. Ibid., pp. 311–312.

6. Theodore H. White, *America in Search of Itself: The Making of the President 1956–1980* (New York: Harper and Row, 1982), p. 165.

7. Ibid., p. 195.

8. Ibid., p. 419.

9. Bernard Berelson, "Communications and Public Opinion," in *Communications in Modern Society*, ed. Wilbur Schramm (Urbana, Ill.: University of Illinois Press, 1948), p. 172.

10. Paul Lazarsfeld, Bernard Berelson, and Hazel Gaudet, *The People's Choice* (New York: Columbia University Press, 1948).

11. Bernard C. Cohen, *The Press and Foreign Policy* (Princeton: N.J.: Princeton University Press, 1963), p. 13.

12. Richard L. Rubin, *Press, Party, and Presidency* (New York: W. W. Norton, 1981), p. 180.

13. Thomas E. Patterson, *The Mass Media Election: How Americans Choose Their President* (New York: Praeger, 1980).

14. Jeff Greenfield, *The Real Campaign: How the Media Missed the Story of the 1980 Campaign* (New York: Summit Books, 1982), p. 15.

Chapter 6

1. Martin Schram, *The Great American Video Game: Presidential Politics in the Television Age* (New York: William Morrow and Company, 1987), p. 184.

2. Alvin Toffler, *The Third Wave* (New York: William Morrow and Company, 1980), p. 445.

3. Ibid., p. 447.

4. John Naisbitt, *Megatrends: Ten New Directions Transforming Our Lives* (New York: Warner Books, 1982), p. 160.

5. Richard S. Hollander, *Video Democracy: The Vote-from-*

Home Revolution (Mount Airy, Md.: Lomond Publications, 1985), p. 106.

6. F. Christopher Arterton, *Teledemocracy: Can Technology Protect Democracy?* (Newbury Park, Calif.: Sage Publications, 1987), p. 161.

7. Ibid., p. 204.

Postscript

1. Everette E. Dennis, David Stebenne, John Pavlik, Mark Thalhimer, Craig LaMay, Dirk Smillie, Martha FitzSimon, Shirley Gazsi, and Seth Rachlin, *The Media At War: The Press and the Persian Gulf Conflict* (New York: Gannett Foundation Media Center, 1991), pp. x, 26.

2. Sidney Blumenthal, *Pledging Allegiance: The Last Campaign of the Cold War* (New York: HarperCollins, 1990), p. 319.

3. Bruce Buchanan, *The Markle Commission on the Media and the Electorate: Key Findings* (New York: The John and Mary R. Markle Foundation, 1990), p. 22.

4. Walter Lippmann, *The Public Philosophy* (Boston: Little, Brown, 1955), p. 126.

5. Paul Taylor, *See How They Run: Electing the President in an Age of Mediaocracy* (New York: Alfred A. Knopf, 1990), pp. 268–269.

6. Theodore H. White, *The Making of the President 1960* (New York: Atheneum, 1961), pp. 3–4.

7. Roger Simon, *Road Show* (New York: Farrar, Straus, Giroux, 1990), p. ix.

8. E. J. Dionne, Jr., *Why Americans Hate Politics* (New York: Simon and Schuster, 1991), p. 355.

Acknowledgments and Annotations

Portions of this book have appeared, in much different form, in the *Review of Politics, Indiana Journal of Political Science, Chicago Sun-Times, Chicago Tribune, Philadelphia Inquirer,* and *St. Petersburg Times.* I am grateful to editors of these publications for their permission to use this material.

James Langford, Director of the University of Notre Dame Press, is an author's model publisher — a continuing source of encouragement and advice as a book takes shape and grows. He was receptive to the idea when it was first proposed, and his interest never flagged. Whatever merit the book might have is largely his.

Most of the interpretations included in the book were originally tested — if not challenged — in classes of the Department of American Studies at the University of Notre Dame. Max Lerner, the youthfully venerable author, professor, and syndicated columnist, occupied the W. Harold and Martha Welch Chair in American Studies at Notre Dame from 1982 until 1984. We collaborated on a course, "Choosing a President in the Media Age," in the spring of 1984, and have worked together on other projects since then. His wise counsel is reflected throughout these pages. As editor of the *Review of Politics*, Thomas J. Stritch, Professor Emeritus of American Studies, proposed a lengthy review-article about the media and contemporary politics. The article that resulted gave direction to my thinking, and Professor Stritch has kindly commented on many of the chapters in this book.

A summer grant in 1989 from Notre Dame's Hesburgh Program in Public Service was valuable in developing a new senior seminar, "Politics, Policy, and the Media," and in working out several points for "The Bully Pulpit at Center Stage" and "The Momentary Majority." I am grateful to Professor David C. Leege, the Director of the Hesburgh Program, for his support and guidance. Roger Skurski, Associate Dean of the College of Arts and Letters at Notre Dame and Director of the Center for the Study of Contemporary Society, generously contributed to publication costs of this volume from funds in the Center's Program on Ethics and the Media.

The route to this book is, I confess, anything but a traditional one. Years of work in journalism, graduate study in English and American Studies, and experience in practical politics and municipal government led serendipitously to Indiana University's Poynter Center for the Study of Ethics and American Institutions, where I coordinated the Center's Citizen and the News Project from 1975 until 1980. Professor William Lee Miller, the former Director of the Poynter Center, is responsible for introducing me to the possibilities of the humanistic treatment of communications and political life.

Notre Dame's Department of American Studies includes journalism as one of its substantive concerns. Since joining the faculty in 1980, I have been able to combine a study of the media with broader cultural analysis, especially our increasingly mass-mediated political culture. Professor Donald P. Costello, Chairman of American Studies during these years, always supported the development of classes and writing projects that explored this territory.

The books referred to throughout the chapters and noted below have been wonderfully useful. I, however, base much of the commentary on reading, watching, and listening to the media coverage of American political life. One can be critical of (and, at times, even infuriated by) messages delivered through the various instruments of popular communications, but what has been called the "daily intelligence" deserves constant scrutiny and appraisal. Husbandly and fatherly gratitude are owed to Judith Roberts Schmuhl and Michael Robert Schmuhl for always permitting observance of the morning and evening rituals with the news — and for understanding that writing a book demands time away from them.

In chapter one, "Smokeless Politics," Nelson W. Polsby's *Consequences of Party Reform* (New York and Oxford: Oxford University Press, 1983) proved valuable in coming to terms with the post-1968 political and media environment. There have been several procedural changes since this book appeared, but it insightfully explains why so many reforms came into being and what they have meant to our electoral system. Theodore H. White's *The Making of the President 1960* (New York: Atheneum, 1961) is justly considered a modern-day classic in political writing. In the last half of the twentieth century, two books stand out for their noteworthy influence on American journalism: *The Making of the President 1960* and *All the President's Men* by Carl Bernstein and Bob Woodward (New York: Simon and Schuster, 1974). White's book made a political campaign a dramatic democratic pageant, worthy of sustained attention by reporters. White took his readers inside the process, and since his book was published hundreds of journalists have followed his path. Woodward and Bernstein also probed the inner workings of a political campaign — but instead of a pageant they found a pigsty. The investigation described in their book continues to stimulate interest for people seeking careers in journalism.

For chapter two, "Image-Making and Anti-Image Journalism," Daniel J. Boorstin's *The Image: or What Happened to the American Dream* (New York: Atheneum, 1962) remains the essential study of how the media can create their own reality, with perceptions the dominant objective and result. The book's subtitle was subsequently changed to *A Guide to Pseudo-Events in America* to emphasize Boorstin's critical point about the contrivance and manipulation that takes place daily in our communications environment. David Halberstam's *The Powers That Be* (New York: Alfred A. Knopf, 1979) and Joe McGinniss's *The Selling of the President 1968* (New York: Trident Press, 1969) offer a wealth of reportage and anecdotes about how people in politics perceive the involvement of the media in our public life. Jimmy Carter's *Why Not the Best?* (Nashville: Broadman Press, 1975) is an excellent example of an autobiography that seeks to convey a specific and appealing political image, with the focus on the person rather than specific policies. The book, which Bantam Books released as a paperback in the spring of 1976, was important in introducing the relatively unknown Carter to the American public. Larry Speakes's *Speaking Out: The Reagan Presidency from Inside the White House* (New York: Charles Scribner's Sons, 1988) is one of several behind-the-scenes accounts of the Reagan White House. It is revealing for what it says about Reagan as president and the journalists assigned to cover this particular presidency. Robert Penn Warren's *All the King's Men* (New York: Harcourt, Brace, 1946) was, of course, inspired by the rise and fall of Huey Long in Louisiana politics in the 1920s and 1930s; however, the novel remains timelessly relevant in its consideration of the conflict between power and ethics and in its treatment of the consequences of knowledge. Michael Novak's *Choosing Our King: Powerful Symbols in Presidential Politics* (New York: Macmillan, 1974) is a probing and stimulating analysis of our political culture, with emphasis on the significance of symbolism in American political life.

In chapter three, "The Bully Pulpit at Center Stage," Jeffrey K. Tulis's *The Rhetorical Presidency* (Princeton, N.J.: Princeton University Press, 1987) cogently traces the emergence of popular leadership by occupants of the White House during the twentieth century. Martin Schram's *The Great American Video Game: Presidential Politics in the Television Age* (New York: William Morrow and Company, 1987) is a revealing journalistic account of television's involvement in the 1984 presidential campaign that raises larger questions about the conduct of contemporary political life. David S. Broder's *Behind the Front Page: A Candid Look at How News is Made* (New York: Simon and Schuster, 1987) is a worthy companion to Walter Lippmann's landmark book *Public Opinion* (1922) in explaining to citizens the intersecting worlds of journalism and politics. Though more personal and less philosophical than *Public Opinion* is, *Behind the Front Page* details the limitations of popular communications and concretely demonstrates the differences between news and truth. The revised edition of George Reedy's *The Twilight of the Presidency* (New York: New American Library, 1987) brings a shrewdly insightful study up to date, making it even more compelling. Garry Wills's *Reagan's America: Innocents at Home* (Garden City, N.Y.: Doubleday, 1987) is not only the most comprehensive and thoughtful study of Ronald Reagan that exists but also a model of how political and cultural analysis can be written. Ronald Reagan's *Speaking My Mind: Selected Speeches* (New York: Simon and Schuster, 1989) brings together some of the memorable statements Reagan delivered throughout his political career as well as his own commentary about the statements. Interestingly, the name Peggy Noonan does not appear in *Speaking My Mind*. In *What I Saw at the Revolution: A Political Life in the Reagan Era* (New York: Random House, 1990), Noonan makes sure everyone knows she wrote several of the major addresses by both Reagan and George Bush. Her memoir tellingly shows the strengths and weaknesses of the relationship between statecraft and stagecraft. Richard E. Neustadt's *Presidential Power: The Politics of Leadership from FDR to Carter* (New York: Wiley, 1980) remains a significant survey of the exercise of executive power in all of its diversity. Richard Nixon's *Leaders* (New York: Warner Books, 1982) includes interesting sketches of world leaders the former president knew as well as his definite (if not always sound) views of leadership today.

For chapter four, "The Momentary Majority," the writing Walter Lippmann did about "the public," the formation of opinion, and the relationship between journalism and public life offers the direction that comes from the articulation of first principles. Of specific, continuing interest: *Liberty and the News* (New York: Harcourt, Brace and Howe, 1920); *Public Opinion* (New York: Harcourt, Brace and Company, 1922), and *The Phantom Public* (New York: Harcourt, Brace and Company, 1925). W. Russell Neuman's *The Paradox of Mass Politics: Knowledge and Opinion in the American Electorate* (Cambridge, Mass.: Harvard University Press, 1986) builds on some of Lippmann's concepts to provide a more refined analysis of the different types of people who make up the public. Walter Dean Burnham's *The Current Crisis in American Politics* (New York and Oxford: Oxford University Press, 1982) probes the "disappearance of the American voter" from the 1960s to the 1980s, and he shows that the decline of our political parties is a prime factor in this disappearance and in the quality of contemporary governance. Kathleen Hall Jamieson's *Eloquence in an Electronic Age: The Transformation of Political Speechmaking* (New York and Oxford: Oxford University Press, 1988) takes a historical and rhetorical approach in explaining the consequences of different means of delivery on the way public figures communicate. Jack Germond and Jules Witcover's *Whose Broad Stripes and Bright Stars? : The Trivial Pursuit of the Presidency 1988* (New York: Warner Books, 1989) chronicles what happened during the 1988 campaign — in public view and behind closed doors.

In chapter five, "Cyclops or Big Bird?" the statements of Jefferson come from *Thomas Jefferson On Democracy*, edited by Saul K. Padover (New York: Hawthorn Books, 1939). James David Barber's *The Pulse of Politics: Electing Presidents in the Media Age* (New York: W. W. Norton, 1980) is more valuable for its historical treatment of the relationship between presidential candidates and the media than its cyclical, paradigmatic interpretation of campaigns in the twentieth century. Theodore H. White's *America in Search of Itself: The Making of the President 1956– 1980* (New York: Harper and Row, 1982) is fascinating, vivid reportage but less compelling in its analysis. Bernard C. Cohen's *The Press and Foreign Policy* (Princeton, N.J.: Princeton University Press, 1963) seems dated in today's media environment; however, several of the study's main points remain pertinent and worth consideration. Richard L. Rubin's *Press, Party, and Presidency* (New York: W. W. Norton, 1981) methodically tracks the three subjects in its title from the eighteenth century to the present. Rubin's conclusions about the effects of communications are reasoned and persuasively presented. Jeff Greenfield's *The Real Campaign: How the Media Missed the Story of the 1980 Campaign* (New York: Summit Books 1982) challenges many of the myths of the media's alleged power by explaining how the 1980 presidential campaign was shaped and influenced by fundamental political realities affecting the electorate.

For chapter six, "Temptations of Technology," the quotations from Alexis de Tocqueville's *Democracy in America* are taken from the translation by George Lawrence and the edition edited by J. P. Mayer and Max Lerner (New York: Harper and Row, 1966). This version of *Democracy in America* includes Lerner's penetrating analytical study, which was published separately in book form, *Tocqueville and American Civilization* (New York: Harper Colophon Books, 1969). Alvin Toffler's *The Third Wave* (New York: William Morrow and Company, 1980) and John Naisbitt's *Megatrends: Ten New Directions Transforming Our Lives* (New York: Warner Books, 1982) gaze into the future and explain what might happen when new forms of technology and our political system converge. In both cases the information they present is more engaging than their speculations. Richard S. Hollander's *Video Democracy: The Vote-from-Home Revolution* (Mount Airy, Md.: Lomond Publications, 1985) surveys the possibility of having citizens involved in public affairs by using their televisions and computer systems. F. Christopher Arterton's *Teledemocracy: Can Technology Protect Democracy?* (Newbury Park, Calif.: Sage Publications, 1987) is a case-by-case investigation of the actual usage by people of some of the new technology that can enhance public knowledge and encourage public involvement. *The Electronic Commonwealth: The Impact of New Media Technologies on Democratic Politics* by Jeffrey B. Abramson, F. Christopher Arterton, and Gary R. Orren (New York: Basic Books, 1988) comprehensively explores "the new media and democratic values," emphasizing that the emerging forms of communications technology could, ultimately, threaten to undermine the foundation of our political and governmental system.

In the postscript chapter to the second edition, "The Theater of War, The War as Theater, and Other Matters," the media involvement in the Persian Gulf War is analyzed in detail in *The Gulf War Reader: History, Documents, Opinions*, edited by Micah L. Sifry and Christopher Cerf (New York: Times Books, 1991) and *The Media at War: The Press and the Persian Gulf Conflict* by Everette E. Dennis, David Stebenne, John Pavlik, Mark Thalhimer, Craig LaMay, Dirk Smillie, Martha FitzSimon, Shirley Gazsi, and Seth Rachlin (New York: Gannett Foundation Media Center, 1991). The 1988 presidential campaign has been the focus of a number of books about the current state of American political life. Three of the most thoughtful descriptions and assessments are Sidney Blumenthal's *Pledging Allegiance: The Last Campaign of the Cold War* (New York: Harper-Collins, 1990), Roger Simon's *Road Show* (New York: Farrar, Straus, Giroux, 1990), and Paul Taylor's *See How They Run: Electing the President in an Age of Mediaocracy* (New York: Alfred A. Knopf, 1990). Bruce Buchanan's *Electing a President: The Markle Commission Research on Campaign '88* (Austin: University of Texas Press, 1991) is a serious academic study of the 1988 election that also includes specific recommendations for citizens, candidates, and the media to improve the conduct —

and content — of campaigns. *Nine Sundays: A Proposal for Better Presidential Campaign Coverage* is a 1991 report by John Ellis for the Joan Shorenstein Barone Center on the Press, Politics and Public Policy at Harvard University's John F. Kennedy School of Government that outlines an ambitious but seemingly workable approach to injecting more substance into presidential campaigns. On the front of the book jacket for the cloth edition of Walter Lippmann's *The Public Philosophy* (Boston: Little, Brown, 1955) is the phrase "On the Decline and Revival of the Western Society." One wonders what Lippmann would have written about the debate over American decline that absorbed so many thinkers and writers following the publication of Paul Kennedy's *The Rise and Fall of the Great Powers: Economic Change and Military Conflict from 1500 to 2000* (New York: Random House, 1987). One wonders, too, what Lippmann might have said about the 1988 campaign. *Why Americans Hate Politics* by E. J. Dionne, Jr. (New York: Simon and Schuster, 1991) is an important book that cogently explains how some of the festering sores on the body politic developed and how they might be treated. That politicians, journalists, and academics now refer to Dionne's argument about the "politics of false choices" with such frequency is a tribute to the book's deserved influence and a sign of hope for the future.